The Damn Good Resume Guide

A Crash Course in Resume Writing

Yana Parker

Ten Speed Press
Berkeley, California

The author wishes to acknowledge her colleagues, friends, and clients,
for their assistance, advice, and contributions to this project.

THANK YOU, people!

10

TEN SPEED PRESS
P.O. Box 7123
Berkeley, California 94707

Distributed in Australia by E. J. Dwyer Pty. Ltd., in Canada by
Publishers Group West, in New Zealand by Tandem Press, in South
Africa by Real Books, and in the United Kingdom and Europe by
Airlift Books.

Cover design by Fifth Street Design
Interior page composition by Jeff Brandenburg, ImageComp
Illustrations by Ellen Sasaki and Akiko Shurtleff

Library of Congress Cataloging-in-Publication Data

Parker, Yana.
     The damn good résumé guide / Yana Parker. — 3rd ed.
          p.   cm.
     Includes index.
     ISBN 0-89815-672-6 (pbk.)
     1. Résumés (Employment)   I. Title.
HF5383.P35   1996
808'.06665 — dc20   96-5132
                                                       CIP

First printing this edition, 1996
Printed in the United States of America

3 4 5 6 7 8 9 10 — 00 99 98 97

CONTENTS

DIRECTOR OF OFFICE OPERATIONS

How I Came to Write
The Damn Good Resume Guide

LONG-TIME INTEREST

For many years I've had a great interest in people's work lives and job satisfaction (including my own) and this first showed up in a three-year volunteer job as director/coordinator of a community Youth Employment Service. That led to a job with an upstate New York community college project to train unemployed high-school dropouts in job-related skills, and then on to a similar position as "Community Worker" with New York State employment offices in Albany, Troy, and Schenectady, a job I really loved.

Later, living in California, I noticed that many of the people in my personal network were involved in career counseling and small business development, and we'd brainstorm and strategize about our own work, just for the fun of it. Then, in 1979, I decided to try self-employment using my writing skills and my new red hot IBM Selectric typewriter. I resigned from office work in the big city to use my talents in a more personally rewarding way. I began by offering an editing, typing, and business-writing service out of my home in Oakland, but soon specialized in resumes, because it turned out to be "a natural" for me, and because very few people seemed to know how to do it well.

THE HUMBLE FREEBIE GETS STATUS

I never really set out to write or publish this book. It started out, in 1980, as just a few loose pages of instructions and examples, handed to clients as "homework" before we'd get together to work on their resume. (I'd grown weary of giving the same instructions verbally over and over, and finally wrote them down.)

In our "Briarpatch" self-help group of small business people there was a financial consultant, Roger Pritchard, and one day I hired him to help me look critically at the fragile economics of my business. He noticed the packet of "homework" pages I gave to clients (by now it included sample resumes and a list of action verbs), and asked "Why are you *giving* this away? Don't you see that it's valuable, and that you could easily get a few dollars for it?"

So I took his advice, and at the same time expanded the packet and wrote up the instructions in greater detail. I designed a card-stock cover, stapled everything together, and priced it at $2. Over the following year it got expanded twice more, and the cover price increased, and I began to suspect that it might be marketable as a how-to guide independently of my resume-writing business. So I typed it up even more carefully, added some graphics, designed a more professional cover, and persuaded two Berkeley bookstores to carry a few copies on consignment.

GETTING PUBLISHED

It turned out that Phil Wood, owner of Ten Speed Press, almost immediately found a copy in Cody's Bookstore, liked it, and proposed publishing it. Out of negotiations with him and senior editor George Young, it became clear that another section would be helpful: answers to the recurrent problems that come up when people attempt to write a resume. So I wrote a section, called "Ten Tough Questions," based on experience struggling with these dilemmas many times over. (That section is now spread throughout the text.) The section on employer acceptance, called "The Acid Test," was developed at the suggestion of Richard Bolles, who pointed out the need to be sure that what was presented really did serve the reader in terms of employer expectations.

Now, over twelve years and three revisions later, *The Damn Good Resume Guide* has clearly become well respected and very popular in its field, with well over half a million copies in print. Professional job counselors call it "the best available," and a fair number of job clubs and career development centers (and even college instructors in business writing, psychology, and women's studies!) use *The Damn Good Resume Guide* as "required reading."

THIS NEW EDITION

The Damn Good Resume Guide first came out in 1983 and was revised in 1986 and again in 1989. Now I have updated it *again* to keep up with changing times and the current needs of job hunters.

This edition has a number of important new features:

- **a clearer and simpler ten-step approach** to resume writing;

- **many more creative solutions** (at each step of the way I have anticipated your "Yes-But's"—problems you may run into in doing *that* step, such as lack of experience or lack of a job target—and provided some creative ideas to resolve them);

- **a new strategy for creating *chronological* resumes** that are as dynamic and interesting as good *functional* resumes;

- **more sample resumes for students and for military personnel** transitioning to civilian jobs.

Many of the features of earlier editions are still in this edition, namely the Action Verbs list, Skill Areas list, Cover Letters, Informational Interviewing, plenty of sample resumes, and The Acid Test: What Do Employers Think?, which I mentioned earlier.

> ▶ **TIP for educators:** I have created two related items to be used in the classroom along with this book, and they are available from Ten Speed Press (see page 79):
>
> - a 24" x 36" **wall poster**, "The Ten Steps" as used in this book, and
> - a **Bookmark-Mini-Guide**, 3" x 8", listing the Ten Steps with a bit more detail. *Get one for each student.*

NOTE: Another group of job hunters—"blue collar" workers—have found very few good examples to help in writing resumes. I have recently published a whole *separate* book just for them called *Blue Collar & Beyond: Resumes for Skilled Trades and Services*, with over 130 sample resumes. (Ten Speed Press, 1995.)

—Yana Parker
Berkeley, CA
Spring 1996

Ten Steps
To Writing a Great Resume

SUMMARY/OVERVIEW

Here's a brief summary of the Ten Steps to writing a great resume:

Step 1: **Choose a job target** (also called a job objective).

Step 2: **Find out what skills, knowledge, and experience are needed** to do that target job.

Step 3: **Make a list of your strongest skills or abilities (say three or four skills)** that make you a good candidate for the target job.

Step 4: **For each key skill, think of several accomplishments** from your past work history (paid or unpaid) to illustrate that skill.

Step 5: **Describe each accomplishment** in a simple, powerful, action statement that emphasizes the results that benefited your employer.

Step 6: **Make a list of the primary jobs you've held, in chronological order.** Include any unpaid work that fills a gap or shows you have the skills for the job.

Step 7: **Make a list of your training and education** that's related to the new job you want.

Step 8: **Choose a resume format that fits your situation**—either chronological or functional.

Step 9: **Arrange your action statements** according to the format you chose.

Step 10: **Summarize your key points at or near the top of your resume.**

NOTE: In REAL-LIFE resume writing, we DO skip around. So *don't worry if YOUR resume comes together in some other sequence! (As long as you do Step 1 and Step 2 first!)*

USEFUL DEFINITIONS

To help us start off on the right foot, here are some DEFINITIONS of terms that will be used throughout this book:

A "DAMN GOOD" RESUME is a **self-marketing tool—a kind of personal advertisement—that shows off your job skills** and their value to a future employer. The main **purpose** of a resume is to **help you get a job interview**. So it starts off by **naming your job target** and then **describes your skills, experience, and accomplishments** as they relate to THAT job target.

Remember, writing a good resume is *very different* from filling out a job application form. **An application form is about JOBS,** and gives just the facts of your employment history. But **a good resume is about YOU** and how you act and perform in your jobs. *It's very important to see the difference!*

A **CHRONOLOGICAL RESUME** presents your work experience in a traditional **by-date** format, listing the jobs you've held and describing the activities and accomplishments of each job in a single paragraph, with the most recent job appearing first.

A **FUNCTIONAL RESUME** presents your work experience by listing the most important **skills** you've used, and then describing a number of activities and accomplishments (drawn from ALL your jobs and life experiences) to document each of those skills.

NOTE: A **Damn Good Resume** can be *either* chronological or functional, because regardless of format it **focuses on a clear job target** and then emphasizes your work/life **accomplishments** to clearly show your unique value to an employer.

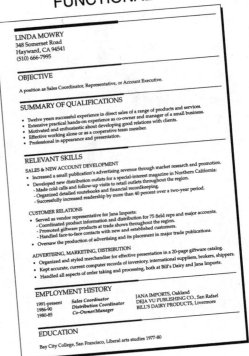

ONWARD TO THE TEN STEPS!

On the following pages you'll find that each of the ten steps is first explained in detail, and then it is followed by "Yes-But's"—some of the problems and dilemmas you may face as you do that step. WHEN the "Yes-But" sounds like YOUR problem, then follow the directions to resolve it. **But if you have no difficulty completing a particular step, IGNORE the corresponding "Yes-But"** and move straight ahead to the next step. *Got it?* Okay, let's GO!

TEN STEPS
To Writing a Great Resume

A Crash Course in Resume Writing

(You can do Steps 3 through 10 in any order, but be SURE to do Step 1 and Step 2 FIRST.)

> **Step 1: Choose a job target**—also called a job objective.

For some people this is the most difficult step, but it's also the most important one! *You can't create a great resume without it.* You need to be able to clearly say what job you want so the reader knows how to evaluate your resume.

A clear job target says to the prospective employer, **"This resume tells you about ME and how I could perform in THIS job."**

Actually, the **job target also helps YOU** to write a great resume, because it **focuses your attention on your goal** and gives you a reference point for choosing the most important things to say about yourself.

For the phrase "Job Target," you could substitute any of these:

- Objective
- Job Objective
- Career Objective
- Career Goal

▶ **HOT TIP: FOCUS**

The people who seem to take the longest time to find a job are often the ones who insist on writing a "generic" resume that lists everything they ever did, or every skill they're interested in using, but fails to focus that information onto a specific job target. They HOPE some employer will figure out what job would fit them . . . but employers can't be bothered; they're looking for people who know what they want.

Step 1: Choose a job target—also called a job objective.

Yes, but . . . "I'm kind of vague about the job I'm looking for; I don't know what I want to do, or CAN do—so I don't know what to put down as my job target."

Okay, then let's take a different approach: Do Steps 2 and 3 *first*, THEN come back to Step 1.

So now *YOUR* first three steps might look like this:

1. **Make a list of your strongest and most favorite skills or abilities (say three or four skills) that you would like to use in your new job.**
2. **Find out what jobs or career areas call for those skills and abilities.**
3. **Choose one of those jobs as your current job target** (or job objective).

(**NOTE:** Steps 4 through 10 stay the same.)

Getting clearer about your job direction is CRUCIAL, and it's not as impossible as you might think. You'll have to take a little time out to do some exploring and find out what you'd really LIKE to do and CAN do. One great way is called **informational interviewing**, described on the following page.

*(I can hear you muttering: **"Don't DO this to me, Yana—I don't have TIME for this stuff."** But without a clear focus on your goal, you can spin in circles endlessly. THAT'S what takes TIME—trust me, I've been there!)*

ABOUT INFORMATIONAL INTERVIEWING

"INFORMATIONAL INTERVIEWING" is a rather fancy phrase for a very straightforward, logical, and extremely helpful NETWORKING idea that helps when you are choosing a career field or clarifying your job objective. Here's what you do:

a. Think back on your most enjoyable days of work (or play), and **jot down some ideas about what you think you're best at and enjoy doing**—not actual job titles, but SKILLS and ABILITIES and TALENTS and INTERESTS—all the things you bring into your various jobs and hobbies.

b. **Ask around** among all your friends, relatives, friends of relatives, neighbors, people you used to work with, ANYBODY, and **get from them the names of people who are already at work using these same SKILLS and abilities that YOU most enjoy using**—somebody you could interview for information (NOT for a job, just for information about that line of work).

c. **Ask** each friend, relative, etc., **for permission to mention THEIR name** when you call the person they have recommended.

d. **Call each of the people** they recommend and:

   - mention the friend or relative's name;

   - **ask for 15 or 20 minutes of their time** to visit with them and learn a bit more about THEIR line of work;

   - **explain that you think you might be interested in that field** because it uses skills and abilities you have, BUT you're not sure yet, you're still checking things out and deciding your direction;

   - **tell them you're not looking for a job yet,** just getting more info to help you get clear.

e. **Make an appointment to** visit them at their workplace for about 20 minutes.

f. **Make up a good list of questions** that you'd like to ask—for example: How did you get this kind of job? What are the requirements for this work? What are the best and the worst aspects of this work? What kind of pay range can be expected in this line of work? What chances are there for moving ahead in this field? Anything that would help you decide whether this is a good direction for you.

g. **Show up right on time** for the meeting, **ask all your questions,** and **take some brief notes** so you won't forget.

h. **Wrap up the meeting on time, thank the person**, and as you leave **ask them for the names of two OTHER people** who use those same skills that you want to use in your next job.

i. When you get home, sit down and **write that person a short thank-you note and mail it right away**.

j. Next day, **call the two people mentioned,** make appointments with THEM, and follow the same plan as above.

k. **Continue this process until you find yourself EXCITED and ENTHUSIASTIC about a particular line of work** and know that this is the direction you want. THEN you'll have a Job Objective you can happily pursue with all your energy.

l. Always keep in mind that **THIS PROCESS WORKS**, and admittedly it **SEEMS a bit scary**, but the fact is that **people ARE willing to share their information** when you show **respect** for their time, **interest** in their line of work, and **appreciation** for their help.

© Damn Good Resume Service

Step 2:	Find out what skills, knowledge, and experience are needed to do that target job.

This step is as crucial as Step 1 because if you DON'T know what's needed, you won't know what to emphasize and what to leave out. So your resume will not do a good job of selling you to an employer, who is looking for people who KNOW the requirements of the job.

> ▶ **TIP:** The main reason people DON'T write effective resumes is that they trip over Steps #1, #2, and #5, that is . . .
> • **They don't choose a clear job target or they don't find out what's required in the new job.** *Already they're off to a bad start!*
> • **They describe all their past jobs** by reciting the **Official Job Descriptions** (b-o-r-i-n-g) **instead of telling what they accomplished** in those jobs, or how they made themselves valuable to their employers by producing good results. This is where the juicy one-liners (Step 5) become essential.
> • **Another reason** people don't write great resumes is that **they FORGET what a resume really IS!** So check out the DEFINITIONS on page 8.

Step 2: Find out what skills, knowledge, and experience are needed to do that target job.

Yes, but . . . "I'm not sure if I even want that job; also I don't have ANY idea how to get that information, short of HAVING the job in the first place!"

The information about *what it takes to do the job* can be found in several ways:

a) In a **classified ad** for the job.
b) In an **employer's job description** for the job.
c) In the **D.O.T.** *(Dictionary of Occupational Titles)* at the local employment office.
d) **From someone already working in that field**.

I highly recommend (d) above—**Informational Interviewing**—as one of the BEST ways to find out exactly what skills the job requires. **Find someone who already does that kind of work.** Visit them on the job or at home, and **ask them to tell you all about "what it takes."**

> **Step 3: Make a list of your strongest skills or abilities (say three or four skills)** that make you a good candidate for the target job.

Here are some examples, taken from several resumes, of skills that others identified as relevant to their target job:

Target job: Service representative for accounting software firm.
Relevant Skills:
Bookkeeping
Teaching/Supervising
Computer Usage
Problem Solving

Target job: Director of a department or special program.
Relevant Skills:
Program Administration
Budgeting/Financial Planning
Personnel Management
Fund-Raising & Public Relations
Counseling

Target job: Position as Health Educator/Nutritionist.
Relevant Skills:
Administration
Supervision & Training
Nutrition Counseling & Health Promotion
Program Development
Public Relations & Community Liaison

Target job: Position as associate in merchandise sales or buying.
Relevant Skills:
Buying
Sales
Negotiating
Counseling/Needs Assessment

Target job: Quality Control Management with the Food, Drug, and Cosmetics Industry.
Relevant Skills:
Quality Administration
Contract Manufacturing
In-house Manufacturing
Management/Troubleshooting
Industry Expertise/Product Knowledge

▶ **TIP**: Having a lot of **specialized knowledge** in your field (for example "Internet WEB Page Design") can be considered the **same as a "relevant skill"** for this purpose. See example in the paragraph above, and more on pages 63–64.

Step 3: Make a list of your strongest skills or abilities that make you a good candidate for your target job.

Yes, but . . . "I don't know what my skills ARE! In a way, I'm good at a LOT of different things, so how do I know what skills to put on my resume?"

Of course you have lots of skills and abilities, but not ALL of them necessarily belong on your resume. **Go back to Step 2 and see what skills are REQUIRED for your Target Job.** Hopefully you have SOME or ALL of those skills, and THOSE are the skills that belong on THIS resume. You may not have ALL of the skills or experience needed, but don't give up: you could be selected for the job anyway, IF you have enough of the basics under your belt and appear to be able to quickly LEARN the remaining skills needed.

If you identify many more skills than are required for the job (and you probably *will!*) resist the urge to put them all on your resume. You may be a great quilter or skateboarder, but those skills **may not be at all relevant to your job objective** and relevancy is the main criterion for what DOES and does NOT belong on your resume.

Also, **Informational Interviewing**—described on page 11—**comes in very handy here;** somebody who is IN a similar job already is in a great position to tell you what skills are useful in any particular field. (See examples on pages 63–64.)

▶ **TIP:** Don't forget your family, friends, work colleagues, and teachers; they may have some valuable insights regarding your skills.

"Work history" in this case means ANY WORK you've done—paid, volunteer, parenting, hobby, *whatever*—that documents the skills and knowledge you need to show for your desired new job.

Examples (taken from several different resumes):

Job Objective: Position as Electronic Sales Representative.

Direct Sales & Product Demonstration

- Set sales record, surpassing all salesmen for any given month in company history.
- Held down company's largest territory; exceeded quotas and greatly increased sales.
- Increased average monthly sales to Pacific Stereo from $1,500 to $13,000.

Job Objective: Position in merchandising display.

Display

- Set up effective retail displays of beverages in supermarkets, liquor barns, liquor stores, and package stores.
- Inventoried and reordered display materials, and maintained warehouse, for Glenmore Distilleries.

Job Objective: Position as Union Representative.

Grievance Handling & Contract Enforcement

- Represented hundreds of grievants covered by diverse contracts.
- Prepared and presented grievances for arbitration.
- Monitored contract agreements through on-going contact with shop stewards and members.
- Represented members in dealings with state & federal agencies.

Objective: Position in public information services.

Information Services/Networking

- Assembled wide range of current job resource materials: newspaper articles on market trends; career magazines and books; job listings; sample resumes.
- Instituted a Job Information Bulletin Board for career-search networking.
- Matched business executives with job seekers in related fields, for the purpose of informational interviews.

Step 4: For each of your key skills, think of several accomplishments from your work history to illustrate that skill.

Yes, but . . . "I can't think of any accomplishments—and anyway, I'm not exactly sure what you *mean* by accomplishments."

Here are some ways to approach this problem:

A. Learn to recognize your accomplishments. They are VERY important, if you want your resume to stand out. Even if you don't have *measurable* accomplishments to put on your resume (such as "Increased sales 40%"), **look at ALL the other evidence of accomplishment** you may have overlooked, such as:

Recognition from your employer:

- **Being asked to take on more responsibility, e.g.,**

    Chosen out of a staff of 15 to train new employees in the clothing department.

    Selected by my manager to handle special and rush assignments.

- **Being awarded an advancement,** a step up in rank, **e.g.,**

    Promoted to senior cargo handler in 1994.

- **Earning a bonus** for bringing in a new customer or maintaining a difficult customer.

- **Getting good feedback on performance evaluations.** You can transform those comments into accomplishment statements, as shown on page 60.

Recognition from other sources:

- **Praise and acknowledgment** from customers, co-workers, outside agencies you contact for your company, union leaders, even competitors.

Here's an example from a flight attendant's resume:

    Received over 100 personal letters of gratitude from passengers served over a 12-year period.

(Solutions above by Rhonda Findling, Vocational Rehab counselor.)

B. Discover some accomplishments through the "P.A.R." approach, one of my favorite techniques. You look at your actions on the job in terms of **PROBLEMS**, **ACTIONS**, and **RESULTS**.

In other words:

— What **PROBLEM** existed in your workplace?

— What **ACTION** did you take to resolve the problem?

— What were the beneficial **RESULTS** of your action?

- Transformed a disorganized, inefficient warehouse into a smooth-running operation by totally redesigning the layout; this saved the company $250,000 in recovered stock.

- Successfully collected thousands of dollars in overdue or unbilled fees by thoroughly auditing billing records and persevering in telephone collection follow-ups.

- Headed off the loss of over a million dollars, due to potential business failure of primary contractor, by negotiating directly with subcontractors.

P.A.R. statements are powerful because they show clear examples of you *making money for your employer*, directly or indirectly, and this should look *very* interesting to your potential *new* employer.

C. Talk to yourself! If you can't think of anything great to say about yourself, **ask yourself the questions below.** Get a friend to listen in or to ask you the questions. This may get your creative juices flowing.

- **Do my co-workers or my boss always count on me** for certain things they know I'm good at? **What, specifically, do they think I'm good at?**

- **If one of my friends at work were to brag about me** to somebody else, what would they brag about? What does that say about my skills?

- **If I had to teach a new employee the tricks of the trade**—that is, teach them how to do a GREAT job in my line of work—**what do I do that's special, that I could teach this new employee?**

- **If I suddenly had to leave the area**—say, to take care of a sick relative—**what would my work buddies miss about me** while I'm gone? How would their jobs be tougher when I'm not there to help?

- **If I had to put together a Training Manual for my job** (or the job I'm now looking for) **how would I describe what it takes to do this job superbly?**

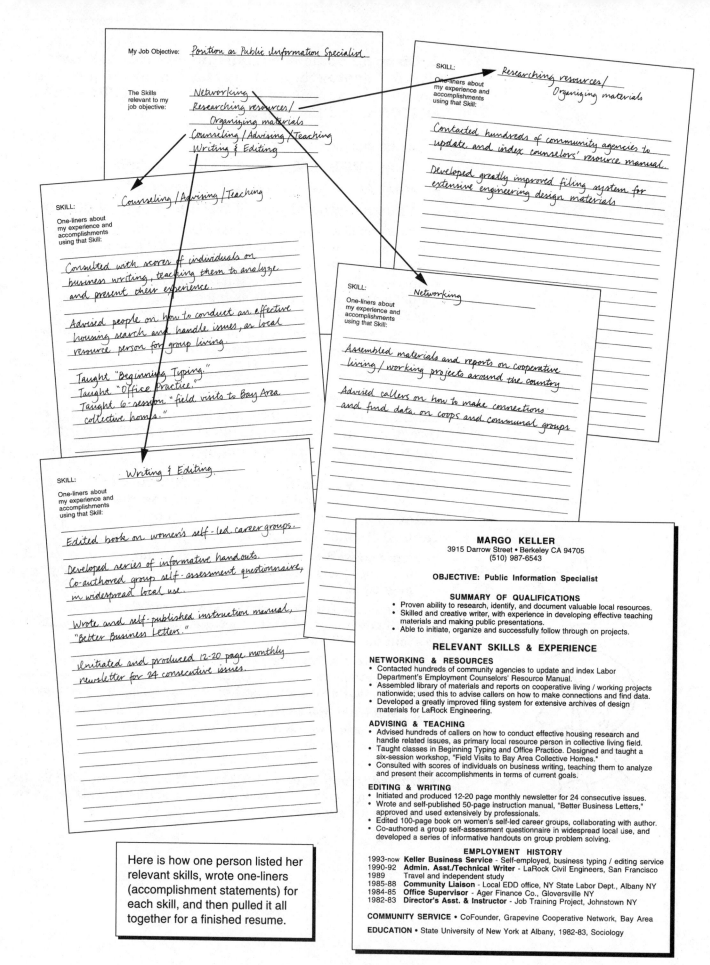

My Job Objective: _Position as Public Information Specialist_

The Skills relevant to my job objective:
- _Networking_
- _Researching resources /_
- _Organizing materials_
- _Counseling / Advising / Teaching_
- _Writing & Editing_

SKILL: _Researching resources / Organizing materials_

One-liners about my experience and accomplishments using that Skill:

Contacted hundreds of community agencies to update and index counselors' resource manual.

Developed greatly improved filing system for extensive engineering design materials

SKILL: _Counseling / Advising / Teaching_

One-liners about my experience and accomplishments using that Skill:

Consulted with scores of individuals on business writing, teaching them to analyze and present their experience.

Advised people on how to conduct an effective housing search and handle issues, as local resource person for group living.

Taught "Beginning Typing."
Taught "Office Practice."
Taught 6-session "field visits to Bay Area collective homes."

SKILL: _Networking_

One-liners about my experience and accomplishments using that Skill:

Assembled materials and reports on cooperative living / working projects around the country

Advised callers on how to make connections and find data on coops and communal groups

SKILL: _Writing & Editing_

One-liners about my experience and accomplishments using that Skill:

Edited book on women's self-led career groups.

Developed series of informative handouts. Co-authored group self-assessment questionnaire, in widespread local use.

Wrote and self-published instruction manual, "Better Business Letters."

Initiated and produced 12-20 page monthly newsletter for 24 consecutive issues.

Here is how one person listed her relevant skills, wrote one-liners (accomplishment statements) for each skill, and then pulled it all together for a finished resume.

MARGO KELLER
3915 Darrow Street • Berkeley CA 94705
(510) 987-6543

OBJECTIVE: Public Information Specialist

SUMMARY OF QUALIFICATIONS
- Proven ability to research, identify, and document valuable local resources.
- Skilled and creative writer, with experience in developing effective teaching materials and making public presentations.
- Able to initiate, organize and successfully follow through on projects.

RELEVANT SKILLS & EXPERIENCE

NETWORKING & RESOURCES
- Contacted hundreds of community agencies to update and index Labor Department's Employment Counselors' Resource Manual.
- Assembled library of materials and reports on cooperative living / working projects nationwide; used this to advise callers on how to make connections and find data.
- Developed a greatly improved filing system for extensive archives of design materials for LaRock Engineering.

ADVISING & TEACHING
- Advised hundreds of callers on how to conduct effective housing research and handle related issues, as primary local resource person in collective living field.
- Taught classes in Beginning Typing and Office Practice. Designed and taught a six-session workshop, "Field Visits to Bay Area Collective Homes."
- Consulted with scores of individuals on business writing, teaching them to analyze and present their accomplishments in terms of current goals.

EDITING & WRITING
- Initiated and produced 12-20 page monthly newsletter for 24 consecutive issues.
- Wrote and self-published 50-page instruction manual, "Better Business Letters," approved and used extensively by professionals.
- Edited 100-page book on women's self-led career groups, collaborating with author.
- Co-authored a group self-assessment questionnaire in widespread local use, and developed a series of informative handouts on group problem solving.

EMPLOYMENT HISTORY
1993-now	**Keller Business Service** - Self-employed, business typing / editing service
1990-92	**Admin. Asst./Technical Writer** - LaRock Civil Engineers, San Francisco
1989	Travel and independent study
1985-88	**Community Liaison** - Local EDD office, NY State Labor Dept., Albany NY
1984-85	**Office Supervisor** - Ager Finance Co., Gloversville NY
1982-83	**Director's Asst. & Instructor** - Job Training Project, Johnstown NY

COMMUNITY SERVICE • CoFounder, Grapevine Cooperative Network, Bay Area

EDUCATION • State University of New York at Albany, 1982-83, Sociology

> **Step 5: Describe each accomplishment** in a simple, powerful **action statement** that emphasizes results that benefited your employer. (This is what I call a **"juicy one-liner."**)

Put the action words at or near the beginning of the line, and be sure to mention specific, provable, successful results whenever possible.

For example, when the skill is Customer Relations, the action statement might be:

- Developed a better approach to providing excellent customer service, which won back many of our old customers and expanded our new-customer base.

> ▶ **TIP:** DON'T mention activities you never want to do again—or you may end up with a job you don't enjoy!

> *Step 5: Describe each accomplishment in a simple, powerful action statement, emphasizing the beneficial results.*
>
> **Yes, but . . .** "I don't know how to write an action statement. What exactly do you mean by an action statement anyway?"

There's a ton of examples in this book and all my other books. A strong action statement tells WHAT YOU DID and what RESULTS you got from your actions. And of course this all has to be relevant to your job target!

Here are some more examples of ACTION STATEMENTS taken from three different resumes:

- Designed and presented hour-long weekly orientation program for career development organization; doubled membership.
- Increased account base by 50% at two locations, through assertive salesmanship and consistent follow-up.
- Developed friendly, supportive, give-and-take relationships with coffee shop patrons, building a loyal base of repeat customers.

Step 6: Make a list of past jobs you've held, in chronological order.

List your most recent job first, then your earlier jobs. Give the dates of employment, the job titles, and the employers. Include any unpaid work (or education) that fills a gap or shows you have the skills for the job.

Here's how it might look:

1995–present	**Dispatcher**	Billingham's Roofing, Oakland
1990–95	**Journeyman Roofer**	Billingham's Roofing, Oakland
1985–90	**Freelance Roofer**	Clients in San Mateo County

OR, like this:

1992–96	**Counter Sales**	Bellarosa Coffee, Chicago
1990–91	**Receptionist**	Elementary School, Chicago
1987–90	**Homemaker & Student**	
1983–87	**Asst. Office Manager**	Crowley Floors, Chicago

Here are some more examples:

EMPLOYMENT HISTORY

1994–present	**Manager, Domestic Operations** SOLUTIONS TO MOVING, INC., Corporate Relocation Services, Charleston, S.C.
1970–94	**Lieutenant Colonel**, UNITED STATES AIR FORCE **Chief, Inspector General**, 1990–94 USAF – Air Transportation **Deputy Director**, 1988–90 USAF – Cargo and Requirements **Chief**, 1986–88 USAF – Cargo Operations

(Job hunter recently in transition from the military)

WORK HISTORY

1994–96	**Part-time/Summer Office Work** ENSR Environmental Engineering, Xerox, Acura, Pennzoil, and Citibank, (through Kelly Services, temporary agency)
1990–94	**Production Assistant, part-time** TEN SPEED PRESS, Berkeley

STUDENT HISTORY: B.A., 1996

1996	CALIFORNIA COLLEGE OF ARTS & CRAFTS, Oakland
1988–92	UNIVERSITY of CALIFORNIA, BERKELEY

(Student just graduating)

EMPLOYMENT HISTORY

1992–96	**Public Relations Rep** NATIONAL TOURIST OFFICE OF SPAIN, San Francisco
1991	**Marketing Coordinator** FEE + MUNSON Architects, San Francisco
1990	**Administrative Assistant** CROWLEY MARITIME CORP., San Francisco

(Job hunter working her way up)

Step 6: Make a list of the past jobs you've held, in chronological order.

Yes, but . . . "This is really tough for me. For one thing I have a lot of little GAPS (and one big one) in my work history. Also, I don't know if I should list EVERYTHING—I'll look like a job-hopper or a flake, with all those short-term jobs! Besides, some of those jobs I'd like to *forget*, they're so unimpressive."

Initially, just to get an overview, list ALL your past jobs; then check below for what to leave in, what to leave out, and what to modify.

WHAT TO INCLUDE . . .

- **Include ALL of your jobs**, however short-term they were, **IF you are very young or you have very little work experience.**

- **Include ALL of the jobs that show experience related to your job objective** even if they were short-term or unpaid.

- **Include jobs that are not particularly related** to your current job goal **IF** they help create a picture of stability, but don't describe them in detail.

- **Include unpaid work** if it helps to prove you have skills and experience or it fills in a gap. See examples on pages 23 and 24.

- You could **include a period of training or education** in your Work History if that helps fill in a gap, as shown on pages 23 and 48.

WHAT TO LEAVE OUT . . .

- **Omit jobs that were very brief UNLESS** they are needed to show how you developed your skills—or to fill in a skimpy work history. Round off your employment dates to years, to avoid creating small gaps.

- **Eliminate the earliest jobs** if you're worried about **age discrimination.**

- **You COULD omit jobs that aren't important to your new goal**—or jobs that create a not-so-great impression—as long as dropping them doesn't leave a big hole in your work history.

> **If you've only had ODD JOBS or short-term work or self-employment,** there are several ways to deal with this, depending on your situation:

- **If you did roughly the same kind of odd job repeatedly,** or for a long period of time, you could **create your own job title and call yourself self-employed.** (In a sense you were, weren't you?) *For example:*

Household Repairman (self-employed) Chicago, 1991-present
(Customer references available on request)
A&S Hauling & Cleaning (self-employed) Chicago, 1991-present
(Customer references available on request)
Child Care (self-employed) Chicago, 1991-present
(Customer references available on request)

Since these **jobs can't be verified** through the normal channels, it will be very important to **find a few people you have worked for who can act as good references.** (See Recommendation Letter Guide on page 65.)

- **If you've done lots of very different odd jobs,** it will be more of a challenge, but the basic idea is the same: **create an appropriate job title** (or titles) and list it just like a regular job. You should pick the odd jobs that you did most often and ignore the others, for simplicity and to make a better impression. Certainly don't mention any demeaning jobs, or jobs you hated, if you can possibly leave them out.

- **If you have been self-employed for quite awhile,** then your work history can't be easily verified just by one phone call. BUT, you can still prove to a new employer that you really DO have the experience, and also a record of reliability, by **detailing specific projects** and **providing good recommendation letters** (see page 65) from past clients and customers.

List the TEMP AGENCY (or agencies) as the EMPLOYER on your resume, and pick one job title that covers *most* of the temp work. Then under that, list the specific assignments, describing the accomplishments, the experience, and the skills gained. **Round off dates.** It could look like this:

1991–92 **Administrative Assistant/Secretary**
KELLEY SERVICES, Atlanta
Assignments & accomplishments:
- Typed business correspondence and routed incoming calls for several busy offices.
- Cleaned up a backlog of past due accounts receivable for Martinson Dry Cleaning.
- Conducted accurate year-end inventory for Graphic Design Studio.

- If you are **CURRENTLY** unemployed, it would help a LOT to **find an immediate short-term opportunity to get some unpaid volunteer work experience**, preferably in your desired line of work, and **put that on your resume now** even if you don't start until next week. This will look better on your resume than being unemployed. But don't use the word "volunteer" to describe this position—*work is work is work!* (Rename the "Employment History" to read "Work History.")

- For any **PREVIOUS periods of unemployment,** think back to what you were actually doing. If you can find **ANYTHING** that could be presented as "work," then create a job title alternative for it that will have the most credibility in the work world. Be realistic, and at the same time **don't buy the idea that certain work "doesn't count." Instead, present that work with dignity.** Here are some examples from several different people's resumes:

1990 **Self-employed Handyman** (4 months)
1991 **Electronics Trainee** - City Vocational Program
1988 **Apprentice Painter** - Moe's Paint Shop, San Bruno
1988 **Full-time Student** - Carlsbad Community College
1983 **Full-time Caregiver** - Home care of elderly parent
1980 **Full-time Parent** - Three small children
1975-83 **Parenting & Community Work** - PTA, Scout Leader

If the **gap in your work history is due to time out for parenting,** here is a way to deal with that with dignity:

Avoid the traditional chronological resume format and **create a functional style resume to emphasize your skills and knowledge.** Customize the Work History to fit your own circumstances. **If you DID do some volunteer work during this period** (even a LITTLE bit) include that in your "Work History" to help fill the gap. For example:

WORK HISTORY

1985-1996   Full-time Parent, plus community work involving Fund-Raising, Voter Registration, and Community Service Committee work.

▶ **TIP:** Some advisors call for pulling out skills from parenting and homemaking. Unless you are *extremely* clever and sophisticated in doing this, I believe it is likely to backfire with most employers. **Unfortunately, we haven't yet arrived at a point in civilization where the work world honors parenting with the respect it deserves.** Until that happy day, dig hard for skills developed *outside* the home, in community work. (Of course, if you luck out and come across an *enlightened* employer, *why not go for it!)*

▶

  TIP: For even more ideas on filling gaps in your work history, see my book, *Blue Collar & Beyond: Resumes for Skilled Trades and Services*, Ten Speed Press, 1995.

This could include correspondence courses, apprenticeships, work-study programs, and relevant workshops. List the name of the school or other place where you trained, the degree or certificate, if any, and the year completed IF it's fairly recent.

You can omit this section IF you have no training, no college experience, and no school courses to list that are in any way related to your new job goal.

"Training" and "Education" could be listed as separate sections on your resume, or (if they are both short) they could be combined into one section.

If you are a member of professional organizations that relate to your job target, you could add a separate section to your resume, called "Professional Affiliations," and place it just below your Education.

Step 7: Make a list of your training and education that's related to the new job you want.

Yes, but . . . "I've done lots of things, but I don't know what to include and what NOT to include. HELP!"

Okay, here are some guidelines:

TRAINING

- If you **completed the training, list just the certificate** you earned.

- If you **only completed PART of the training** (or you didn't get a certificate or diploma) **list every course you took** that is **directly related** to your current job target.

- If you are **new in the field, list every course you took** that is related to your current job target—even if you DID complete the training.

EDUCATION

- If your **education goes beyond high school, include any academic credentials and your degree,** even if they aren't directly related to your job goal. Generally, in this case, you'd omit mention of high school.

- You can **mention your college work even if you don't plan to get a degree.** Here are some ways to show it:

  - Liberal Arts, Laney Community College, Oakland CA
  - Accounting Major, 1991-92, Brooks College
  - Business Classes, Reno Community College, Reno
  - Business Classes, 1987, Reno Community College: Accounting, Financial Planning, Sales & Marketing
  - Correspondence coursework in the military, equivalent to A.A. degree in electronics.

- **Don't mention a high school diploma UNLESS** your new job specifically calls for it and you have no other schooling or job-related training to put on your resume.

- If you have **no job-related training,** and you recently left high school, **you could list any courses you took in school that show your interest** and commitment to this job goal. List the courses under a heading called "Related Education."

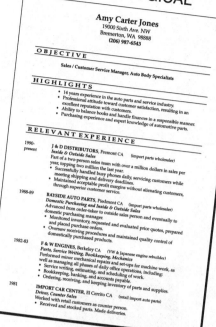

CHRONOLOGICAL

Amy Carter Jones
19000 Sixth Ave. NW
Bremerton, WA 98888
(206) 987-6543

OBJECTIVE

Sales / Customer Service Manager, Auto Body Specialists

HIGHLIGHTS

- 14 years experience in the auto parts and service industry.
- Professional attitude toward customer satisfaction, resulting in an excellent reputation with customers.
- Ability to balance books and handle finances in a responsible manner.
- Purchasing experience and expert knowledge of automotive parts.

RELEVANT EXPERIENCE

1990-present **J & D DISTRIBUTORS**, Fremont CA (import parts wholesaler)
Inside & Outside Sales
Part of a two-person sales team with over a million dollars in sales per year, topping two million the last year.
- Successfully handled busy phones daily, servicing customers while meeting shipping and delivery deadlines.
- Maintained acceptable profit margins without alienating customers, through superior customer service.

1988-89 **BAYSIDE AUTO PARTS**, Piedmont CA (import parts wholesaler)
Domestic Purchasing and Inside & Outside Sales
Advanced from order-taker to outside sales person and eventually to domestic purchasing manager.
- Monitored inventory, requested and evaluated price quotes, prepared and placed purchase orders.
- Oversaw receiving procedures and maintained quality control of domestically purchased products.

1982-83 **F & W ENGINES**, Berkeley CA (VW & Japanese engine rebuilder)
Parts, Service Writing, Bookkeeping, Mechanics
Performed minor mechanical repairs and set-ups for machine work, as well as managing all phases of daily office operations, including:
- Service writing, estimating, and scheduling of work.
- Bookkeeping, banking, and accounts payable.
- Ordering, receiving, and keeping inventory of parts and supplies.

1981 **IMPORT CAR CENTER**, El Cerrito CA (retail import auto parts)
Driver, Counter Sales
Worked with retail customers as counter person.
- Received and stocked parts. Made deliveries.

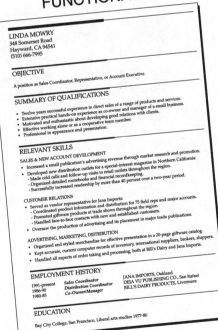

FUNCTIONAL

LINDA MOWRY
348 Somerset Road
Hayward, CA 94541
(510) 666-7995

OBJECTIVE

A position as Sales Coordinator, Representative, or Account Executive.

SUMMARY OF QUALIFICATIONS

- Twelve years successful experience in direct sales of a range of products and services.
- Extensive practical hands-on experience as co-owner and manager of a small business.
- Motivated and enthusiastic about developing good relations with clients.
- Effective working alone or as a cooperative team member.
- Professional in appearance and presentation.

RELEVANT SKILLS

SALES & NEW ACCOUNT DEVELOPMENT
- Increased a small publication's advertising revenue through market research and promotion.
- Developed new distribution outlets for a special-interest magazine in Northern California:
  - Made cold calls and follow-up visits to retail outlets throughout the region.
  - Organized detailed routebooks and financial recordkeeping.
  - Successfully increased readership by more than 40 percent over a two-year period.

CUSTOMER RELATIONS
- Served as vendor representative for Jana Imports:
  - Coordinated product information and distribution for 75 field reps and major accounts.
  - Promoted giftware products at trade shows throughout the region.
  - Handled face-to-face contacts with new and established customers.
- Oversaw the production of advertising and its placement in major trade publications.

ADVERTISING, MARKETING, DISTRIBUTION
- Organized and styled merchandise for effective presentation in a 20-page giftware catalog.
- Kept accurate, current computer records of inventory, international suppliers, brokers, shippers.
- Handled all aspects of order taking and processing, both at Bill's Dairy and Jana Imports.

EMPLOYMENT HISTORY

1991-present *Sales Coordinator*   JANA IMPORTS, Oakland
1986-90   *Distribution Coordinator* DEJA VU PUBLISHING CO., San Rafael
1980-85   *Co-Owner/Manager*   BILL'S DAIRY PRODUCTS, Livermore

EDUCATION

Bay City College, San Francisco, Liberal arts studies 1977-80

Step 8: Choose a resume format that fits your situation.

(Chronological if you're staying in the same field and you have an unbroken employment history; or **Functional** if you're making a career change OR you don't have a continuous record of paid employment).

Here's the essential difference between a FUNCTIONAL resume and a CHRONOLOGICAL resume:

"Chronological" means your work experience is arranged in order by *dates* of the jobs you've held (usually the most recent first)—this is the traditional way of arranging a resume, and places more emphasis on your JOB TITLES and your employment history.

"Functional" means your work experience is described by emphasizing the SKILLS involved—putting the descriptive details into skill-group paragraphs in a separate "Relevant Skills" section above your bare-bones chronological list of jobs.

CHRONOLOGICAL	FUNCTIONAL
JOB TITLE #1 -something I did in that job -something I did in that job	RELEVANT SKILL #1 - something I did using that skill - something I did using that skill RELEVANT SKILL #2
JOB TITLE #2 -something I did in that job -something I did in that job	- something I did using that skill - something I did using that skill RELEVANT SKILL #3
JOB TITLE #3 -something I did in that job -something I did in that job	- something I did using that skill - something I did using that skill Job Title #1 Job Title #2 Job Title #3

Step 8: Choose a resume format that fits your situation, either Chronological or Functional.

Yes, but . . . "I can't decide which format to choose and it's driving me crazy!"

Don't worry; either format could work if done well. So if you can't make up your mind which format is best for you, start out with a **functional** resume. That will keep you focused on the **skills** that are relevant to your desired NEW job.

▶ **TIP:** Remember to mention briefly, in each action statement, *when and where* the accomplishment happened, so your experience is clear and believable.

A functional format could be especially useful if your RELEVANT skills—the skills required for your NEW job target—**are not so obvious** when someone looks only at your chronological job history.

For example: If you developed skills through a hobby or volunteer work and you now want to use those skills in a *paid* job, those skills might not even show up in a chronological resume format but they could be made OBVIOUS in a functional format where you're not limited to describing your activities under job titles.

If you're feeling in an experimental mood you could **try out BOTH formats**, chronological and functional, to see which one "feels right."

Keep in mind that **a chronological format is particularly useful if you are staying in the same field and moving up** to the next level of responsibility, because it clearly shows your job progression. And this format is **preferred by some employers in more conservative fields** such as finance and law.

However, traditional chronological resumes, with their wordy and predictable job descriptions *can* be

SO BORING. Here is a **new strategy for putting some ZIP and PIZZAZZ into a chronological resume:**

1. **Replace** the tediously long job-description paragraph with **two or three brief descriptive sentences** that concisely describe your essential role and activities in the company, including the level of your responsibility.

2. **Follow up** that brief job description by listing (for each job) **a series of your most impressive accomplishments that show how you distinguished yourself on that job.** Choose accomplishments that are particularly **relevant to your NEW job goal**, and in each case point out just what you did and how your actions benefited your employer.

With this strategy you **allocate MOST of the space on your resume for the information that the employer REALLY needs and wants to see.**

Of course your overall work history, your range of experience, and your education and training are all vitally important, *but they're not sufficient in themselves* for getting invited to an interview. It's your **record of valuable contribution and your uniquely effective work habits** that make the big difference.

A **good example** of a chronological resume created with this new strategy can be found on page 44.

Step 9: **Arrange your action statements** from Step 5 according to the format you chose.

If you chose a **chronological** format, place each action statement **under the appropriate job title** where the action happened;

OR . . .

If you chose a **functional** format, place each action statement **under a skill category.** (The key skills you listed in Step 3 can now become your skill categories.)

> Step 9: Arrange your action statements from Step 5 according to the format you chose.
>
> **Yes, but . . .** "What if I change my mind about which format to use?"

If you change your mind, you can RE-organize the *same* one-liners into another format. For example, if you started out with a **functional resume**, your data might look something like this:

RELEVANT EXPERIENCE

Writing & Editing
- Wrote feature articles for national magazines, including ALL ABOUT BEER, as No. California field editor and photojournalist.
- Another one-liner or two.

Photography
- Produced product shots, location, and personality photos for ALL ABOUT BEER magazine.
- Another one-liner or two.

THEN, if you decide that the **chronological resume** would really work better, you could rearrange the one-liners in a chronological format, and it might look something like this:

EMPLOYMENT HISTORY

1982-90 **Writer/Photographer** ALL ABOUT BEER magazine
- Wrote feature articles on all aspects of home-brewing.
- Produced product shots, location, and personality photos.

Later you will need to get some feedback from someone working in the field, and you can ask them which format seems to work best for you.

The examples above illustrate the difference between the two basic formats, chronological and functional. It's also made clear in the definitions on page 8, and in the little diagrams on page 27.

Step 10: Summarize your key points at or near the top of the resume.

Now, for the icing on the cake, look over your resume and gather the most relevant strengths and features of your experience.

Make a brief list—say, four to six short lines—of key points that the new employer will need to know and that will make you look attractive and qualified for the new job.

This list should appear under a heading called "Summary" or "Highlights." You could also name this section anything else that is descriptive, such as:

- Summary of Qualifications
- Highlights of Qualifications
- Professional Profile
- Qualifications

Put that summary list at the top of the resume just below your "job target," and set each statement off with a bullet.

> ▶ **TIP:** It's great if you can keep each summary statement to one line.

Here are a couple of examples of Summaries from other people's real resumes:

SUMMARY
- Thirteen years experience in purchasing and scheduling.
- Outstanding customer service skills.
- Consistently evaluated as an excellent employee.
- Able to build strong working relationships with co-workers.
- Won three "Ideas in Action" awards for cost-cutting proposals.

(Job target was Customer Services Assistant/Scheduler)

SUMMARY
- Top-notch administrator with 15 years experience in finance.
- M.B.A. plus extensive training through in-service seminars.
- Outstanding productivity as both loan officer and supervisor.
- Unique combination of expertise in mortgage banking, training, sales, and finance.
- Dynamic leader and team builder, consistently motivating others toward success.

(Job target was Director of Training)

In this book's resume examples you'll find a lot of consistency in what we have chosen to include in a Summary. However, WHATEVER WORKS is a good guideline! You don't have to do it MY way if you have a better idea, but the recommendations listed on the next page will certainly assure you of a strong Summary.

Step 10: Summarize your key points at or near the top of the resume.

Yes, but . . . "I don't know what to put in the Summary."

A good summary could include:

- **Number of years or months of experience** in the job target field.

- **Your education**, training or certification in that field.

- **An accomplishment** or recognition that "says it all," if possible.

- **Your key skills, talents, or special knowledge** related to this job.

- **Something about your personal work style or attitude** toward the job that would look appealing to an employer.

To be sure you've selected good Summary statements, ask:

- **Is every item in the Summary *relevant*** to my job target?

- **Have I *supported* all the Summary statements** through my one-liners in the body of the resume?

REMINDERS for wrapping up your resume:

- **Proofread** for grammar and punctuation.

- **Check the spelling** with your word processor's spell-checker, or check the spelling carefully by hand. **If you're not an *excellent* speller, get help from someone who is!**

- **Get feedback** from someone in-the-know. Ask them to review your resume and give you their honest opinion of its effectiveness.

24 Sample Resumes

These are all actual resumes of real people with whom the author or another "damn good resume writer" has worked. Nothing has been made up, but some of the names, dates, and details have been changed to protect the privacy of the job hunter.

Resumes written by writers other than the author have been identified in a credit line at the bottom of the resume.

GENERAL

STUDENTS

MILITARY TRANSITIONS

MARIA DOSHAN

4408 Cedar Lake Road • Santa Rosa, California 95401
(707) 888-6754

Objective: Position as **Health Plan Marketing Trainer.**

Committed to the educational process, guiding students to achieve mastery of skills and realization of their own goals and objectives.

HIGHLIGHTS OF QUALIFICATIONS

- 7 years professional experience in seminar design and delivery, including facilitation of an employee training program.
- Keen intuition; warm, sincere, down-to-earth teaching style.
- Special talent for creating an environment conducive to learning.
- Effective team member who is comfortable with leading or collaborating.
- 10 years experience in successful health care marketing.

REPRESENTATIVE SKILLS & ACCOMPLISHMENTS

PROGRAM DEVELOPMENT & PRESENTATION

- Designed and presented **seminars** for hospital middle managers on the effective use of various management reports:
  …**developed learning materials** (handbooks, exercises, reading lists, audio-visuals, evaluation forms);
  …assisted managers in increasing department productivity and cost efficiency.
- **Developed** and delivered group **presentations at national, regional, and local** conferences for health care professionals, on productivity measurement.
- **Presented an overview on marketing** to senior employees for Education and Training Department's "Reorientation" program.

TRAINING

- **Created and conducted** on-going quarterly **training programs** for non-professional health care staff, consistent with Medicare standards for home care.
- **Trained** nurses, respiratory therapists, and pharmacists on appropriate use of pharmaceutical products.
- Chosen as participant **trainer at four annual sales conferences,** to share successful sales strategies with colleagues.
- **Performed and taught** creative dramatics; **trained educators** on the use of creative dramatics in the classroom.

SALES & MARKETING EXPERTISE

- Earned **sales achievement award** for 3 consecutive years:
  …produced largest single sale of new clients from a multi-hospital system;
  …retained client base without loss, for 2 years (the only representative to accomplish this).
- Delivered **highly successful sales presentations** to employer groups, outlining Kaiser benefit package, and contributing to a major membership increase (+2400).
- Researched and presented a **marketing assessment** for Kaiser Medical Center, well received by joint administrative team and department chiefs.

– Employment History and Education on Page Two –

MARIA DOSHAN
Page Two

Maria got feedback from the employer that her resume was one of the best among 40 applications for the job. Maria's cover letter is on page 67.

EMPLOYMENT HISTORY

1995–present	**Health Plan Representative**	KAISER PERMANENTE
1990–94	**Sales Consultant**	AMERICAN HOSPITAL ASSN., Chicago, IL
1989–90	**Marketing Director**	MEDICAL HOME CARE, Chicago, IL
1987–88	**Sales Representative**	DORSEY LABORATORIES, Chicago, IL
1986–87	**Sales Representative**	TEXAS PHARMACEUTICAL, Chicago, IL
1986	**Supervisor**	KELLY SERVICES, Chicago, IL
		Interviewed and tested job applicants.
1984–85	**Instructor, Dramatics**	CLIMB, INC., Chicago, IL

EDUCATION & PROFESSIONAL DEVELOPMENT

B.A., with honors, **Education/Theater Arts** – UNIVERSITY OF CHICAGO, 1984

- Time Management Seminar 1996
- Negotiation Skills 1995
- Persuasive Selling Skills 1992/1995

JOHN J. REED
421 Jasper Alley
San Francisco, CA 94133
(415) 937-0099

Objective: Entry level position as electronics engineering technician, involving field service and/or research and development.

SUMMARY OF QUALIFICATIONS

- Very strong commitment to developing a career in electronics.
- Productive and responsible; willing to learn and handle any tasks needed.
- Skill in tracing schematic diagrams, analyzing circuits, trouble-shooting problems.
    … Heald College training as Electronics Engineering Technician.
    … Two years as Army radio mechanic and instructor in radio repair.
- Over 20 years experience in successfully dealing with customers.
- Able to represent a company with a professional appearance and manner.

RELEVANT SKILLS & EXPERIENCE

Electronics Knowledge

- Completed 2-year course at Heald College, in Electronics Engineering Technology.
- Completed math, physics, and drafting courses at City College:
    …Algebra …Geometry …Trigonometry …Calculus …Physics …Drafting
- Taught radio repair in US Army Signal Corps.
- **Rebuilt and rewired** electrical home appliances.
- **Replaced portion of house wiring**, bringing it up to code.

Trouble-Shooting/Research

- **Researched** in technical manuals and consulted with professionals in the field, to resolve technical problems in home/auto repair; experience in use of hand tools in wood-working and metal-working.
- **Diagnosed problems** in home electronics: TVs, radios, CD players, tape decks.

Customer Relations

- Developed a successful, professional approach to providing **top quality customer service**, consistently applying these principles:
    …Create an atmosphere that encourages the customer to freely express complaints;
    …Thoroughly and tactfully research the potential solutions to their problem;
    …Get feedback to be sure the customer is, in fact, satisfied with the results.

EMPLOYMENT HISTORY

1976–present	**Waiter** – ROHDALE'S RESTAURANT, San Francisco
1991–95	**Consultant** to Restaurant Management Part-time (concurrent with above); advising management on personnel problems and professional standards in restaurant service.
1974–76	**Field Radio Repairman & Instructor** – U.S. ARMY SIGNAL CORPS

EDUCATION & TRAINING

Graduate, HEALD COLLEGE, Electronics Engineering Technician
US ARMY, Field Radio Repair

JOSEPHINE TELLER

325 Hillegass Blvd.
Berkeley, CA 94705
(510) 987-6543

Objective: Position as Supermarket Checker or Head Clerk.

SUMMARY OF QUALIFICATIONS

- 15 years experience in the grocery industry, as head clerk, checker, and cashier.
- Excellent reputation with customers as a competent, knowledgeable, and helpful professional.
- Enjoy my work and consistently greet customers with a smile.
- Honest, reliable, and productive.

RELEVANT SKILLS & EXPERIENCE

CUSTOMER SERVICE

- Developed a reputation for **excellent customer service** by:
  …acknowledging the customer's presence and making eye contact;
  …greeting customers in a friendly manner, and giving them full attention;
  …taking time to answer a question or find someone else who could.
- Served as **product expert** on sophisticated items, directing customers to:
  …exotic spices and ingredients …ethnic foods …unusual gourmet items.
- **Increased sales** in the higher-profit Natural Foods Department (and increased customer satisfaction) by **advising customers** on bulk alternatives to name-brand items.

SUPERVISION

- As Head Clerk, **managed "front end"** of the store:
  …**Prepared daily schedules** for staff of up to 18 clerks, to assure maximum check stand coverage at all times;
  …**Assigned staff** to cover peak hours and continuous stocking.
- **Trained** new clerks.

ADMINISTRATIVE

- **Balanced checker's cash drawer** with consistently high level of accuracy.
- As **Office Cashier** for one year:
  …accurately balanced books and balanced deposits
  …answered phones …prepared daily sales report …made deposits
  …processed returned checks …prepared monthly sales report for HQ.

EMPLOYMENT HISTORY

1981–present	Retail Clerk, journeyman	CO-OP SUPERMARKET, Berkeley, CA
1980	Buyer's Assistant	LILLY department store, Oakland, CA
1975–79	Manager's Assistant	WALLACE Clothing Store, Spokane, WA

EDUCATION

Business Classes, 1979 – SPOKANE COMMUNITY COLLEGE

ROBERT VALLARTA
1224 Seymour Avenue
Richmond, CA 94805
(510) 987-6543

Objective: Position as Park Supervisor with regional park district.

SUMMARY OF QUALIFICATIONS

- Over 25 years professional experience in horticulture, developing excellent knowledge of landscaping and plants.
- Lifelong interest and background in gardening.
- Excellent working relations with the public, and with co-workers and employees of all ethnic groups.
- Proven record of reliability and responsibility.
- Skill in planning, coordinating and supervising projects.

RELEVANT EXPERIENCE

SUPERVISION, TRAINING, SAFETY

- As Landscape Maintenance Supervisor at Conland:
  ...**supervised and scheduled** 35 permanent gardeners and 6 foremen;
  ...**trained and evaluated** the above employees, teaching safe use of power tools, principles of horticulture, and chemical pest control.
- **Supervised** 20-40 CETA gardeners, both youth and adults:
  ...presented **safety guidelines** at mandatory weekly safety meetings;
  ...followed-up and **monitored attendance** and **productivity**;
  ...**taught** proper use of equipment and tools;
  ...**taught** pruning techniques, weed control, turf management;
  ...organized and planned field trips to botanical sites.
- **Trained and supervised** hundreds of seasonal gardening helpers, students at U.C. Berkeley working at Botanical Gardens.
- CPR and First Aid Certificate.

PARK TECHNICAL EXPERIENCE

- Operated all **equipment and power tools**:
  ...walk mowers   ...riding mowers   ...lawn edgers   ...lawn vacuums
  ...generators   ...tractors   ...chain saws   ...weed eaters   ...brush cutters
  ...rotary reel and gang mowers   ...turf equipment and attachments
  ...gas and electric trimmers.
- **Maintained** grounds and greenhouses at U.C. Berkeley Botanical Gardens, involving:
  ...small engine repair ...concrete construction ...paving ...excavating
  ...tree removal ...slide repair ...erosion control ...plumbing ...drain cleaning
  ...fertilization ...rototilling ...sod lawns ...pest control ...irrigating ...planting
  ...mowing lawns ...pruning ...special soil ...maintenance of athletic fields
  ...sprinkler system installation ...greenhouse construction
  ...grading (residential, commercial) ...industrial lot cleaning
  ...chemical applications (weed control) ...repair of patios/driveways/foundations
- **Maintained** school district truck; excellent driving record.
- **Maintained** indoor plants at Conland and school administration offices.

– Continued on page two –

Retired after 30 years as a gardener with the school district, Robert now is applying for a position with the regional park district.

RELEVANT EXPERIENCE, Continued

ADMINISTRATION

- Submitted daily **reports** to Conland, following inspection of work sites, damage, equipment and materials needed, and tasks remaining to be done.
- **Interviewed** and **hired** gardeners for Conland.
- **Verified** and submitted weekly employee **time-sheets** for both CETA and Conland.
- **Coordinated** field trip arrangements for CETA workers: selected botanical sites to visit, and rearranged work schedules to accommodate special trips.
- Developed estimates for Conland landscape **contracts**.
- **Organized** retirement dinners for School District gardeners.
- Served on **negotiating** team for union contracts with Oakland School District.

LIAISON, COMMUNITY RELATIONS

- **Led tours** of Botanical Gardens for student groups and garden clubs.
- Acted as **liaison** between gardeners and administrators, as union shop steward at Oakland Unified School District.
- Served as **liaison** between CETA gardeners, District teachers, and administrators.
- **Mediated** minor grievances and approved landscaping requests of Homeowners Association, as landscape maintenance supervisor for Conland contractors.

EMPLOYMENT HISTORY

1982–95	**Gardener/Assistant Foreman**	OAKLAND UNIFIED SCHOOL DIST.
	Gardener Caretaker, live-in	" " Chabot Science Center
1980–82	**Landscape Maintenance Supv.**	CONLAND, Landscaping Division, Concord (building contractors)
1979–80	**Head Gardener**	BROOKSIDE HOSPITAL, San Pablo
1968–79	**Nurseryman**	BOTANICAL GARDENS, U.C. Berkeley

EDUCATION & TRAINING

Horticulture course work, MERRITT COLLEGE:
- Horticulture • Greenhouse Management • Plant Diseases • Herbicidious Plants
Horticulture Workshops, U.C. Berkeley BOTANICAL GARDENS:
- Plant Identification • Plant Maintenance • Propagating • Spraying
Supervisory Training, OAKLAND SCHOOL DISTRICT

RUBEN PEREZ

999 Center Drive, San Francisco, CA 94123
(415) 987-6543 home • (415) 876-5432 office

Objective: Position as High School Principal.

EDUCATION

M.A., **School Administration**, UNIVERSITY OF THE PACIFIC, Stockton, CA
B.A., History and Physical Education, UNIVERSITY OF THE PACIFIC

Lifetime **Teaching Credentials**: General Elementary and Secondary
Lifetime **Administrative Credentials**: Standard, Elementary, and Secondary

PROFESSIONAL AFFILIATIONS

Association of California School Administrators
United Administrators of San Francisco

SUMMARY OF QUALIFICATIONS

- 19-year background in administration, at State Department of Education, high school, and university levels.
- Experience in all aspects of high school operations: curriculum development, academic department head, dean of students, personnel evaluation, master schedule building.
- Effective principal of a large comprehensive high school (ADA 2300), comprising a very diverse ethnic population.
- A creative and "take-charge" type administrator; proven ability to see what needs to be done, and do it.

PROFESSIONAL EXPERIENCE & ACCOMPLISHMENTS

Assistant Principal   HARRISON HIGH SCHOOL, San Francisco, CA
1993–present   BUSHNELL HIGH SCHOOL, San Francisco, CA

- Developed a **successful plan for dropout prevention** featuring one-on-one instruction for truant and high-risk students. **Results**: …eliminated disruptive classroom behavior …reduced after-school detention …upgraded the educational atmosphere …increased revenues for ADA.
- **Recovered over $200,000 in ADA revenues** for the school district: Restructured work schedule of the attendance technician to provide needed time and facilities for documenting legitimate absences.

1991–93 **Management Intern**   AMFAC CORP., Food Division, Morgan Hill, CA

- Trained staff and developed personnel for middle management positions.

1989–91 **Director, Special Projects**   CENTRAL SCHOOL DISTRICT, Sacramento, CA

- Oversaw implementation and evaluation of federal and state special projects and programs for the District.

– Continued on page two –

Ruben's resume shows how you can focus on your unique achievements rather than job descriptions even when using a CHRONOLOGICAL FORMAT Ruben's cover letter is on page 68.

PROFESSIONAL EXPERIENCE & ACCOMPLISHMENTS
(continued)

1986-89 Principal   NORTH HIGH SCHOOL, Sacramento, CA

- Initiated the **updating of course descriptions and expansion of course offerings**, to accommodate the needs of both low achievers and gifted students.
- **Originated** and coordinated a highly successful **"Career Day"** program,which:
  –provided students an in-depth exposure to a wide range of occupations;
  –helped teachers to relate their classroom subject matter to the world of work.
- **Spearheaded a successful fund-raising drive** to replace antiquated lighting for school football field, raising $30,000 through a specially-arranged carnival.
- **Coordinated the joint efforts** of parents, students, community business leaders, and city officials to support this project.
- **Increased ADA revenues** by $45,000 by initiating an in-school study hall program which tremendously reduced class-cutting.
- Effectively **reduced youth gang activity on campus** by bringing together a task force of parents and community representatives, including state legislators and local law enforcement agencies.
- **Initiated** the formation of a **minority student club** to increase participation in campus activities. **Results:**
  –raised self-esteem and enhanced image with other students;
  –elected the first Hispanic female student body president;
  –developed a stabilizing force for working with youth gangs;
  –involved minority students in sponsorship of a popular annual talent show.
- Won recognition for providing **outstanding and effective leadership**.

1976–78 Asst. Principal, Curriculum   SOUTH HIGH SCHOOL, Salinas, CA
- Developed and coordinated **Master Schedule**.
- Chaired the District's Student Attendance Review Board.
- Represented my high school on District Professional Curriculum Committee.

1972–76 Educational Consultant   STATE DEPT. OF EDUCATION, Sacramento, CA
- Led instructional team in the **development and review of curriculum** for educationally disadvantaged students statewide.
- Oversaw disbursement of $18.3 million for compensatory education programs statewide.

1969–72 Project Director   UNIVERSITY OF THE PACIFIC, Stockton CA
- Coordinated and developed a pilot program funded by the federal government which entailed development of a GED curriculum for high school dropouts; recruited and placed students into college, job training programs, and jobs.

KATE DIETRICH
4877 Twin Oaks Road
Berkeley, CA 94707
(510) 885-9090

Kate aims for an accounting job that allows her to apply knowledge of computers. Kate's cover letter is on page 67.

Objective: Position with a microcomputer firm, in accounting/bookkeeping.

HIGHLIGHTS OF QUALIFICATIONS

- Over 12 years experience in accounting, taxation, and administration for a variety of businesses.
- Over 4 years full-charge bookkeeping experience with computerized accounting systems.
- Familiar with both PC-DOS and Macintosh operating systems.
- Exceptionally organized and resourceful, with a wide range of skills.
- Reliable and adaptable; learn new systems quickly, and take initiative.

RELEVANT EXPERIENCE & ACCOMPLISHMENTS
Accounting/Bookkeeping

- Handled full-charge bookkeeping for 20 accounts monthly at a CPA firm: calculated payroll taxes, sales taxes, financial statements, depreciation schedules, and Schedule C for each firm.
- Developed a broad base of experience in bookkeeping for a range of businesses including auto repair facilities, service industries, wholesale manufacturing, retail stores, and property management.
- 12 years accounts payable experience. Solely managed up to $75,000 a month in accounts payable.
- Extensive experience preparing payroll for up to 60 employees on a weekly basis; computed, prepared, paid and filed all federal and state tax returns.
- Conducted extensive research of source documents to accurately construct a corporation's first year financial statement and general ledger.

Computer Expertise

Accounting

- Maintained accounting records for 20 businesses, using a custom accounting package on a WANG computer. Generated financial statements, payroll taxes, and W-2 forms.
- Generated financial statements and general ledger for a retail corporation, using New England Business Systems accounting package.

Systems & Applications

- Used LOTUS 1-2-3, WordPerfect and MS WORD for spreadsheets and correspondence.
- Used dBase to design custom screens, generate reports, design menus, and design program sub-routines.
- Used Microsoft WORKS and MS WORD to generate spreadsheets and correspondence.
- Generated coding and entered data for output to a photo-typesetter.

EMPLOYMENT HISTORY

1994–present	**Administrative Assistant***	DOUGLAS HILL, Attorney, Berkeley
1994–present	**Bookkeeper/Office Manager***	GRIFFIN MOTORWERKE, Berkeley
1993	**Customer Service Rep**	COLORCRAFT, Inc. (printing), Milwaukee, WI
1992	**Quality Control Assistant**	M.C.P. Co. (printing), Milwaukee, WI
1989–91	**Full Charge Bookkeeper**	EDWIN DONAHUE, CPA, El Cerrito
1983–88	**Bookkeeper/Parts Manager**	AUTOWERKE, Inc. (auto repair/parts), Berkeley
	* concurrently	

EDUCATION & TRAINING

A.A., with honors, **Printing and Publishing Operations**, Milwaukee Area Tech. College, 1993; **dBase**, Vista College, Berkeley; **Concepts of Data Processing, Accounting,** U.C. Extension, Berkeley

DENNIS CLEAVER

223 SE Saiquist Rd.
Prescott, OR 97048
(987) 654-3210

Job Objective: Customer Service Manager

SUMMARY

- Ten years of customer service experience.
- Imaginative problem solver with exceptional organizational skills.
- Ability to plan, initiate, and carry out ideas and programs.
- Bilingual in English and German.

PROFESSIONAL EXPERIENCE

PELHAM GRAPHICS, INC., Portland, OR   1986–present
Customer Service Manager
Supervised department of four employees. Directed the distribution of products and services to increase sales. Resolved serious collection and customer service problems.

- Reorganized filing systems and flow of information, resulting in substantially improved cash flow for company.
- Managed Just-In-Time inventory system for nine regional distribution centers, resulting in $20,000 savings over one-year period.
- Set up four distribution centers in the U.S. and one in the U.K., including training of personnel in product and logistics of paper flow.
- Created and implemented weekly open order reports, improving on-time deliveries by 32%; on-time delivery consistently stayed at 98% to 100%.
- Scheduled responsibilities and cross-trained customer service and inside sales staff.
- Trained employees in developing and maintaining good customer relations, effectively negotiating and resolving problems.
- Oversaw record keeping involving order entry, invoicing, accounts payable, complaint handling, and reports.

QVC CORPORATION, Portland, OR   1983–1986
Administrative Assistant
- Relieved Purchasing Manager of daily details.
- Prepared and maintained log of purchase orders written by all buyers.
- Compiled and wrote weekly and monthly reports for corporate office.
- Coordinated and scheduled weekly meetings and transcribed minutes.

EDUCATION

A.A. (Business College), Private Handelsschule of Ingolstadt, Germany
Additional courses: • Supervisor Development • Statistical Process Control
• The Role of Supervisor in Employee Relations
• Stephen Covey's "Seven Habits of Highly Effective People"

COMPUTER SKILLS

• Lotus 1-2-3 • Professional Write • MRP/OMAR

PROFESSIONAL AFFILIATIONS

Member of International Customer Service Association

Resume written by Dislocated Workers Project, Portland, Oregon

STEVEN RICHARDS

23 Darlington Court
Portland, OR 97201
(987) 654-3210

Objective: Senior position in credit management.

SUMMARY

- Eighteen years experience in secured, open account, and lease financing.
- Expertise spans all facets of credit management within a major corporation.
- Team player with ability to make sound business decisions in stressful environments.

PROFESSIONAL EXPERIENCE

Brothers Leasing Corporation, Portland, OR   1995–present
SR. PORTFOLIO ADMINISTRATOR

Former national equipment leasing company. Administered all credit and collection activity involving a $15 million runoff portfolio.
- Consistently maintained collections within company standards.
- Met or exceeded all personal/company goals established.

Miracle Leasing Corporation, Portland, OR   1992–1995
REGIONAL CREDIT MANAGER

National equipment leasing company. Managed a credit team which processed $34 million in business, including investigation, financial analysis, and documentation.
- Trained financial and credit analysts in company policy which created uniformity in credit approval throughout organization.
- Sound decision making allowed for 15-20% higher volume and lower delinquency rate of all regional teams.
- Credit authority increased from $35,000 to $100,000 within one year.

Kinny (Division of George-Winters), Portland, OR   1992
WEST COAST CREDIT MANAGER

National manufacturer of steel rolling doors for commercial use and wood doors for residential housing. Managed all credit and collection activity involving $2 million accounts receivable portfolio in eight western states.
- At very critical point, assumed position of General Credit Manager at national headquarters.
- Lowered days sales outstanding from 63 to 47 days.
- Created new credit function for West Coast under new decentralized structure.

Carrel Financing, Inc., Portland, OR   1980–1991
DISTRICT CREDIT MANAGER

National equipment financing company. Managed a $10 million portfolio, including credit investigation, collections, repossession, and bankruptcy.
- Consistently maintained top 20% of collections nationwide.
- Total responsibility for repossessing all equipment in two states; arranged for pickup, inspection, maintenance and repairs in preparation for successful resale.
- Credit authority increased from $10,000 to $100,000.

EDUCATION

B.S., Business, Portland State University, Portland, OR

Resume written by Dislocated Workers Project, Portland, Oregon

LORRAINE CHAPMAN

7855 West End Avenue
Lafayette, CA 94549
(510 987-6543)

Objective: **Position as a research assistant, legislative advocate, and/or press aide with a public policy organization.**

SUMMARY OF QUALIFICATIONS

- Strong communication and research skills.
- Successful in promoting an organization and generating funding.
- Willing and able to handle a wide variety of tasks.
- Creative, resourceful, and thorough in developing a project.

EMPLOYMENT / RELEVANT EXPERIENCE

1995-present *Administrative Asst.* – MATT KURLE INC., IMPORTER/DISTRIBUTOR, Orinda, CA

Jan-Aug 1994 *Current Affairs Research Intern* – KQED PUBLIC TV, San Francisco, CA

COMMUNICATION & RESEARCH SKILLS

- **Investigated program topics** for "Express" show and "MacNeil/Lehrer NewsHour," involving extensive library research and interviewing.
- **Negotiated with government and private agencies** for data and film footage.
- Summarized research and **prepared informational packets** for producers.
- **Pre-interviewed** studio guests. **Wrote position papers** for show moderator.

1992-93 *Assistant Director* – **ASUCD STUDENT FORUMS**, U.C. Davis

PROGRAM DEVELOPMENT – MEDIA/PUBLICITY

- **Collaborated on the planning, promotion**, and production of 30 public lectures (total audience 32,000); speakers included Geraldine Ferraro, author Alice Walker, physicist Edward Teller:
  - **Corresponded** with prospective speakers and scheduled appearance dates;
  - **Organized event logistics**: seating, security, decor;
  - **Coordinated and scheduled publicity**; prepared advertising budget.
- **Conceived and produced a comprehensive TV program** on AIDS which was tied in with community AIDS Awareness Week:
  - **Won funding** of $2,000 for the project through written and oral presentations;
  - **Wrote press releases**, PSAs, advertising copy; worked with graphic artists on design of customized promotional materials;
  - **Secured media coverage** and re-broadcasting of the event on community TV;
  - Earned commendations from university administration and City of Davis.

FUND-RAISING & COMMUNITY RELATIONS

- **Successfully won support and funding** from campus and civic organizations through a variety of means:
  - **Met with organizational directors** to present program ideas and needs, securing donations of services: catering, limousine services, publicity.
  - **Coordinated and promoted fund-raising receptions** attended by civic leaders, generating significant funds for ASUCD and broad media coverage.

EDUCATION

B.A. Economics, cum laude, University of California, Davis, 1994
Education Abroad Program – Tokyo, Japan, Summer 1994

BRADLEY FRENCH

P.O. Box 900
San Rafael, CA 94915
(415) 459-2008

Job objective: Writer/Photographer/Editorial Assistant position with a newspaper, magazine, PR firm or book publisher.

SUMMARY OF QUALIFICATIONS

- Successfully published writer, editor and photographer.
- Enthusiastic and committed; a go-getter who doesn't quit until the job is done right.
- Effective problem solver; a thorough researcher.
- Well organized and focused in coordinating projects.

RELEVANT EXPERIENCE & ACCOMPLISHMENTS

WRITING & EDITING

- Wrote feature articles for national magazines, including *ALL ABOUT BEER*, as Northern California field editor and photojournalist.
- Wrote KQED Beer Festival Guide for *San Francisco FOCUS* magazine's 1992 issue.
- Created and published a local specialty newsletter for home brewers/collectors:
  – Pub and book reviews;
  – Local events and openings;
  – New products and recipes.
- Selected, proofread and copyedited manuscripts for Stonehenge Books.

PHOTOGRAPHY

- Published photographs for:
  – Magazines: produced product shots, location and personality photos, for *ALL ABOUT BEER* Magazine;
  – Newspapers: photo series on Ann Rice, well-known local author, in *FICTION MONTHLY*;
  – Book: "The Elitch Gardens Story," published by Rocky Mt. Writers Guild, Boulder, CO;
  – Slide show: Sierra Club's national slide show, "The Ultimate Environmental Issue;"
  – Photographed models for glamour and fashion for Vannoy Talent Agency.

PUBLISHING & PR

- Implemented successful marketing campaigns for Jack London books at Star Rover.
- Headed promotion and PR department for Stonehenge Books, Denver book publisher:
  – Arranged media interviews for new authors; initiated a new weekly radio program featuring interviews with Stonehenge authors;
  – Organized book-signing publicity events in area book stores;
  – Wrote press releases and submitted review copies to book columnists;
  – Developed mail-order book promotion directed toward special interest groups.

EMPLOYMENT HISTORY

Current	*Writer/Photographer*	FREELANCE; most recent assignments for: *NETWORK MARKETING; PRACTICAL WINERY; AMATEUR BREWER.*
1991–95	*Field Editor, No. Cal.*	ALL ABOUT BEER MAGAZINE, Anaheim, CA
1992–94	*Book Sales Rep.* *(concurrent with above)*	STAR ROVER HOUSE, book publisher, Oakland
1990–91	*Book Sales Coord.*	DETERMINED PRODUCTIONS, SF, books/toys/gifts mfg.
1989–90	*Editing/Mktg. Asst.*	STONEHENGE BOOKS, book publisher, Denver, CO

EDUCATION & TRAINING

KIIS Broadcasting Workshop, Hollywood, CA
FCC 3rd Class License
B.A., Anthropology – Arizona State University; Tempe, AZ

CARLENE DOONAN

2731 Southgate Drive
Berkeley, CA 94702
(510) 525-9934

Since Carlene has no paid experience as a baker, she makes note of all her courses in cooking.

OBJECTIVE

A position as apprentice baker, with opportunity for increasing levels of responsibility.

SUMMARY OF QUALIFICATIONS

- Work hard, learn fast, willing and able to assume responsibility.
- Passion for food; commitment to producing highest quality products.
- Experience with successful retail design and display.
- Good team player; work well with all kinds of people.

EXPERIENCE

Cooking Knowledge

- Studied with master chef, Ken Wolfe, learning:
  – Principles and techniques of food preparation;
  – Importance of quality and freshness of ingredients;
  – Chemistry and effects of combining ingredients;
  – Coordinated timing of food preparation;
  – Innovative approaches to traditional cooking principles;
  – Balancing flavors within a dish and within a meal.

Coordination/Teamwork

- Maintained and supervised a balanced flow of inventory for theatre food concession and for retail gift store:
  – Monitored sales including seasonal fluctuations;
  – Researched to determine best prices, by phone and at trade shows;
  – Assured correct stocking and display.
- Coordinated timing and priority of tasks, as store manager.
- Worked on a finely tuned sales team to expedite customer services.

Speed/Accuracy

- Handled large volume of customers in minimum time, selling theatre tickets and selling retail merchandise.
- Accurately counted, recorded and deposited cash receipts for retail store.
- Prepared puff pastry dough in cooking class, consistently completing in record time.

WORK HISTORY

1988–present	**Store Manager**	MIASMA gift store, Berkeley
1985–88	**Assistant. Mgr.**	" " "
1984–85	**Theatre Manager**	RENAISSANCE-RIALTO THEATRE GROUP, Berkeley
1983–84	**Clerk/Counter Sales**	" " "

EDUCATION

Laney College, 1982–85 Liberal Arts
Classes in Cooking Principles with Ken Wolfe, Master Chef

CHRISTIANE LLOYD

980 - 43rd Avenue
San Francisco, CA 94121
(415) 459-6906

OBJECTIVE

Position as language instructor in German, preferably including:
- academic counseling;   – design of teaching materials;
- curricula development;   – course evaluation.

SUMMARY OF QUALIFICATIONS

- 5 years' experience teaching German at all levels to many different target groups.
- Strong practical and theoretical background in developing and selecting appropriate teaching materials.
- Successful and self-confident in classroom presentation and team teaching.
- Proven effectiveness in program design and administration.
- Certified trainer for student teachers.

RELEVANT ACCOMPLISHMENTS

CLASSROOM TEACHING

- Taught German as a Second Language in a variety of settings:
  - Beginning, intermediate and advanced students;
  - Male offenders in a correctional institute;
  - Female Spanish-speaking residents of Germany;
  - Foreign laborers in employment advancement courses.

COUNSELING/TRAINING

- Trained student teachers in the classroom, and conducted seminars focusing on didactic issues.
- Advised adult immigrant students on complex personal and academic issues:
  - immigration and employment regulations;   – housing and landlord concerns;
  - entrance exams and class level placement;   – health and medical resources.

CURRICULA DEVELOPMENT & COURSE EVALUATION

- Improved existing curriculum on German as a Second Language, incorporating more diversity to respond both to needs and interests of students and to knowledge gained from academic research (focused on rules of grammar and on speaking/reading/writing/listening comprehension).

WORK HISTORY

1992–present	**Teacher/Language Instr.**	HAMBURG VOLKSHOCHSCHULE, German as a Second Language Dept., Hamburg, Germany
1990–91	**Nurse Substitute/Driver**	ANSCHARHOHE EPPENDORF NURSING HOME, Hamburg, Germany
1983–90	**Full-time student** **Substitute Nurse, part-time**	UNIVERSITY OF HAMBURG, Germany

EDUCATION & CREDENTIALS

German equivalent of Masters Degree
Credentials to teach students through 10th grade
(First examination for intermediate school teachers, through 10th grade)
Relevant coursework: German, Pedagogic, Politics

LARRY B. ELTON
2330 Blake Street
Berkeley, CA 94704
(510) 437-4288

Objective: Senior position in engineering management.

HIGHLIGHTS OF QUALIFICATIONS

- Business oriented; able to understand and execute broad corporate policy.
- Strength in analyzing and improving engineering and administrative methods.
- Effective in facilitating communication between management and project team.
- Proven ability to manage both large and small groups and maintain productivity.
- Successful in negotiating favorable design and construction contracts.

RELEVANT EXPERIENCE & SKILLS

MANAGEMENT

- Developed innovative, cost-effective concept in project management of specialty chemical plant, assigning the design engineering to outside contractors.
- Supervised recruitment and staffing of over 40 project team professionals.
- Wrote detailed execution plans for major design and construction projects, involving:
  - project staffing;   – preliminary schedule;   – preliminary cost estimate;
  - engineering drawings;   – construction contractor selection;   – definitive cost estimate;
  - approvals of contractor construction plans.
- Wrote comprehensive summary for senior level management, incorporating monthly reports from specialty engineering, project engineering, and construction management.

CONSTRUCTION MANAGEMENT

- Wrote 800-page Construction Management Guide documenting standardized construction procedures and reporting.
- Increased productivity 12% by introducing a popular 4-day/48-hour work week alternative.
- Successfully headed off loss of over a million dollars, due to potential business failure of primary contractor, by negotiating directly with subcontractors.

ENGINEERING / PRODUCT DEVELOPMENT

- Conceived and patented highly profitable design for a Refrigerant Recovery System which realized a profit of over $15 million in a period of 5 years.
- Trained 25 skilled salespeople to effectively demonstrate patented equipment to various industries.

EMPLOYMENT HISTORY

1989–present	*Project Manager*	ATLANTIC RICHFIELD CO., Walnut Creek, CA
1987–89	*Project Manager*	ALLIED CHEMICAL CO. (now Allied Signal), Morristown, NJ
1984–86	*Project Engineer*	SUN OIL CO. (now Sun Co.), Philadelphia, PA
1977–84	*Engineer*	PENNWALT CORP., Philadelphia, PA
1974–77	*Captain*	U.S. Army Infantry

EDUCATION & TRAINING

B.Sc. Ch.E., Chemical Engineering – UNIVERSITY OF WASHINGTON, Seattle, WA
Graduate studies – PENNSYLVANIA STATE UNIVERSITY and TEMPLE UNIVERSITY

JULIE FRISBEE FORD, M.A.
– Career Development/Vocational Consulting –
2909 McClure Street, 2nd Floor, Oakland, CA 94609
(510) 893-3700

As a professional consultant, Julie places her job objective immediately below her name.

PROFESSIONAL EXPERIENCE

Project Management

Established and managed a vocational consulting firm, Ford and Company, specializing in private vocational rehabilitation:

- **Developed overall job-search strategies, as case manager** for the job-placement phase of clients' rehabilitation plans, contributing to re-employment of hundreds of clients.
- **Designed effective systems** for accomplishing project goals, in the context of a small team of co-workers. Orchestrated the allocation of people, time, and resources, successfully completing projects within industry time-frames.
- **Built an in-house resource library** of up-to-date materials, including:
  …an extensive file of current Bay Area job listings   …employer directories
  …labor market statistics   …career development publications
  …comprehensive files on specific occupations and local employers.

Labor Market Research and Analysis

- **Conducted hundreds of labor market surveys**, identifying: …job availability
  …hiring criteria …salary ranges …physical requirements …job duties …labor market trends.
- Developed **realistic and practical recommendations** for a range of career options, incorporating the results of the labor market surveys.

Vocational Evaluation and Assessment

- **Interviewed clients and documented their personal histories**: educational, avocational, and occupational, **maintaining an objective and impersonal approach**.
- **Administered career development instruments** (paper-&-pencil, and computer-aided):
  …Strong Interest Inventory …Livermore Achievement Motivation Process (LAMP)
  …SkillScan …Myers-Briggs (Personality) Type Indicator …Career Values Card Sort
  …Realistic Assessment of Vocational Experiences (RAVE).
- **Interpreted tests and integrated results** with other relevant factors.
- **Wrote comprehensive official reports** of findings, meeting strict industry criteria.

Counseling

- **Counseled job-seekers,** both on a **one-to-one** basis and in **workshop** settings, with an emphasis on **empowering them to take charge** of their own job search.
- **Worked effectively with a wide range of clients** during their career changes:
  …voluntary and involuntary clients   …cooperative and uncooperative clients
  …industrially injured workers   …dependent spouse in divorce proceedings.

EMPLOYMENT HISTORY • EDUCATION • AFFILIATIONS

1982–Present	**Career Development Consultant**	Ford and Company, Oakland, CA
1973–81	**Mgr., Accts. Payable/EDP Liaison**	Stauffer Chemical, San Francisco, CA
1970–72	**Educator, Adult Education**	Washington Irving School, Syracuse, NY
1969–70	**Educator**	Family Service Center, Syracuse, NY

M.A., Career Development, John F. Kennedy University, Orinda, CA, 1988
B.A., Sociology, Syracuse University, Syracuse, NY, 1970

California Association of Counseling and Development • Bay Area Career Consortium
American Society of Training and Development • California Assn. of Rehabilitation Professionals

CHARLES BOOKMAN

964 Ellsworth Avenue
Oakland, CA 94611
(510) 652-9876
(510) 652-9999 Fax

Objective: Position as Project Manager, Associate Manager, or Consultant, in Marketing, Product Development, Special Projects.

PROFILE

- Over **twenty years professional experience:**
  - 7 years in marketing management in the software industry;
  - 4 years as a Special Projects Officer;
  - 10 years as a licensed Private Investigator.
- **A creative visionary,** equally comfortable collaborating in a team effort, working independently, or directing others.
- **Jack-of-All-Trades** with a wide range of skills from marketing and public relations to product design/development, production management, technical writing, and information gathering & analysis.
- **Proven ability to take charge of a project**, identify and resolve problems, and bring the project to a close.

PROFESSIONAL EXPERIENCE & ACCOMPLISHMENTS

As North American Marketing Manager and U.S. rep for Marvel, developed our previously unknown astronomy program to the position of market leader:

- **Represented** Marvel Multimedia to its business partners in the U.S. in support of their **sales and marketing** efforts.
- **Presented products** at trade shows, to buyers, store managers and consumers.
- **Coordinated advertising and public relations.**
- **Developed strategic business relationships**, leading to higher market visibility and expanded business opportunities.

As Marketing Director for Universe Software, developed the company's product to position as leading astronomy software on the Macintosh:

- **Created product development strategy**.
- Collaborated in the **product specification** of the software.
- **Developed creative branding** for both company and products.
- **Managed sales:** set up accounts with distributors and other outlets, including a program for educational site licensing and sales.
- **Managed public relations**, including announcements, reviews, advertising.

WORK HISTORY

1994–present	**Marketing Manager** – MARVEL MULTIMEDIA, London, England
1988–94	**Marketing Director** – UNIVERSE SOFTWARE, San Ramon, CA
1984–88	**Special Projects Officer** – U.S. COAST GUARD, Alameda, CA
1974–84	**Licensed Private Investigator** – for Personal Injury Attorneys
1967–89	**Officer**, U.S. Coast Guard Reserve – retired as Commander

EDUCATION

J.D., Lincoln University, San Francisco, CA, 1976
B.A., Psychology, San Diego State University, 1967 (Minor: Physics; Math)

JULIA SMITH

Please contact me at (510) 987-6543, during the hours of 8am–7pm.

SERVICES I CAN OFFER:

- Baby sitting
- Lawn mowing
- Raking leaves
- Car washing
- Pet cleaning & grooming
- Pet sitting (feeding & walking)

Baby Sitting:

For the last seven years I have taken care of children from age 10 months to 10 years old. Responsibilities included: cooking; clean-up; feeding and clothing children; ensuring children are home at the correct time; providing breakfast and making bagged lunches; and getting children ready for school.

Car Washing:

I am careful when washing cars and make sure that both the inside and outside of the vehicle are clean, vacuumed and dusted.

Lawn Mowing:

Last summer I earned all of my spending money by mowing lawns. I do a thorough job of mowing, raking and weeding lawns.

Pet Care:

I am experienced in bathing dogs and cats. I love animals and have a dog and three cats, and have washed and clipped my golden lab-retriever. I enjoy pet "sitting" both dogs and cats.

Raking Leaves:

I have some experience raking leaves, and I love autumn.

VOLUNTEER EXPERIENCE:

1994–95: **Volunteer Teacher's Assistant**, Ms. Jean Richards' Grade 5 Class, Smithton Elementary School, Campbell River, B.C. Assisted students with reading, writing and math lessons.

1991: **Volunteer Model,** Modern Hair Salon, Campbell River, B.C. Modeled hair styles.

INTERESTS:

Water and snow skiing, other outdoor sports. Participated in Grade 3-8 Track and Field activities. I enjoy gymnastics and choir, also.

Resume written by Cory Beneker

KRISTIN STERNBERG

1342 Kellogg Court
Alpharetta, Georgia 30202
(404) 987-6543

OBJECTIVE

A position in public relations utilizing my sales experience, communication skills, and leadership abilities.

EMPLOYMENT HISTORY

The Atlanta Journal/Constitution-Advertising Department
Account Executive, October 1995–present
Inside Sales Representative, June 1994–October 1995
Sales Assistant, September 1993–June 1994
- Created and presented several advertising proposals and campaigns, including readership, circulation, and demographic statistics.
- Developed and designed advertising strategies and layouts for my accounts.
- Contacted and collaborated with clients, reviewing and correcting advertisement proofs.
- Gained experience with word processing and Macintosh computer applications.
- Earned award for "Salesperson of the Month," based on sales revenue and new business development.

Atlanta Dogwood Festival
Communications Intern, April–August 1993
- Planned special events and coordination for a volunteer recognition program.
- Recruited and managed several volunteers for the festival.
- Assisted with media and public relations activities, including development of press kits.

March of Dimes Birth Defects Foundation
Pubic Relations Intern, Winter 1992–1993
- Created and prepared a press kit, including press releases, fact sheets, photos, and brochures for promotion of a pre-WalkAmerica event.
- Wrote press releases for the March of Dimes, 1991 community service grants.

Georgia State University
Public Relations Chairman, (Sorority) 1991–1993
- Created and produced a monthly newsletter including the layout and copy.
- Wrote press releases related to chapter activities and initiated members.
- Served as volunteer and chapter liaison for the Children's Miracle Network Telethon.
- Wrote campus news, sorority news, and editorials for *The Signal* newspaper.

EDUCATION & TRAINING

Georgia State University, 1993
B.A., Journalism; Public Relations emphasis

HONORS & ACTIVITIES

- Gwinnell Chamber of Commerce
- Ad 2 Club
- Atlanta Journal/Constitution "Salesperson of the Month" and "Quadrella" winner, achieving 1994 holiday goals.

Resume written by the job hunter

KATHY UYEN

7382 Grand Avenue
Concord, CA 94520
(510) 987-6543

OBJECTIVE

Peer Counselor with focus on developing a bridge for students of different cultures.

HIGHLIGHTS

- Top-notch student experienced in dealing with a wide range of cultures.
- Unique combination of expertise in working with the community and with professional groups.
- Dynamic leader and team-builder, consistently motivating others to succeed.

EXPERIENCE AND ACCOMPLISHMENTS

1995–present **Assistant Counselor** – CENTER FOR NEW AMERICANS, Concord:
- Plan and coordinate peer counseling workshops for junior high school students;
- Cross-cultural translation and interpretation for County Mental Health, and Department of Social Services;
- Counsel cross-cultural girls between the ages of 12–19 from the New American Girls Program;
- Recruit girls from different schools for the American Friends Program;
- Run two peer support groups for teens in the New American Girls Program.

1995–present **President** – FUTURE BUSINESS LEADERS OF AMERICA, Mount Diablo High School Chapter.

1994–1995 **Secretary** – FUTURE BUSINESS LEADERS OF AMERICA, Mount Diablo High School Chapter.

1994 **Teacher's Assistant** – CONCORD CHILD CARE CENTER, Concord:
- Cared for children between the ages of 5 months to 4 years old;
- Coordinated different types of art sessions.

EDUCATION

Mount Diablo High School, Concord, CA; currently a Junior, GPA 4.0.

References available upon request.

Resume written by the job hunter

Ben Nation

987 - 12th Avenue • Santa Cruz, CA 95062 • (408) 987-6543

OBJECTIVE   **Technical Writing Intern**

HIGHLIGHTS
- Excellent written and verbal communication skills.
- Strong technical background.
- Experienced team worker.
- Quick learner.

EDUCATION
- University of California, Santa Cruz: 9/93–present.
- Computer Engineering Major.
- National Merit Scholarship Semifinalist: 1993.

EMPLOYMENT
- Computer Consultant at UCSC's computer labs: 2/95–present.
- Software Test Engineer at Touch Communications: 6/95–9/95.
  – Evaluation: "…learned very rapidly…persistent in solving seemingly hopeless problems…improved our productivity …incredible initiative…worked well with everyone…"
- Designed and maintained personalized computer database for Surf Berkeley: 9/91–9/93.
- Wrote a personal organization program for *JumpDisk Software* magazine: 3/92.

RELEVANT COURSEWORK
- Abstract Data Types: present.
- Introduction to Computer Organization: present.
- Introduction to Logic Design: Winter '96.
- Technical Writing for Computer Engineers: Winter '96.
- Introduction to Programming in C: Spring '95
- Composition and Rhetoric: Spring '95. Evaluation: "…an excellent job of explaining the technical aspects…deep and widespread knowledge of computers…careful to make sure a non-technically versed reader could follow…superior results."
- Introduction to Data Structures: Fall '95.
- Introduction to Programming in Pascal: Fall '94
- Berkeley High School – Computer Programming 1 & 2: Spring & Winter '90; Pascal 1: Spring '93.
- UC Berkeley – Introduction to Pascal: Summer '89.
- Numerous math classes: Algebra; Geometry; Calculus; Discrete Math; Linear Algebra; Engineering Math; Logic.

ORGANIZATIONS
- American Mensa, Ltd.: 1995–present.
- IEEE, UCSC Chapter: 11/94–present.
- COAC, Committee for Open Access Computing: 12/94–present.
- CAUG, Campus Amiga Users Group: 10/94–present.

References available upon request.

Resume written by the job hunter

TODD JAMISON

224 Crocker Avenue • Owen Sound, Ontario N4K N48 • (205) 987-6543

OBJECTIVE: Apprenticeship as a heavy duty equipment mechanic.

SUMMARY OF QUALIFICATIONS

- Effective team player, conscientious worker.
- Experience on several group construction projects.
- Repaired and operated chain saws, lawn mowers, weed-eaters, circular saw, and woodsplitter.

SUMMER WORK EXPERIENCE

1996 *General Labourer/Mechanical Assistant,* MUNICIPAL ROADS DEPARTMENT
- Performed minor equipment repairs.
- Assisted in the clearing of new road allowance.
- Proved myself to be a conscientious, reliable, and resourceful worker while assisting in the development of a new sanitary landfill site at Cape Croker.

1995 *Parks and Maintenance Worker,* COUNTY PARKS & PUBLIC MAINTENANCE
- Assisted in the repairs of small engines and equipment.
- Operated a variety of equipment in the performance of park duties.
- Maintained lawns and gardens for cemeteries and for senior citizens.
- Proposed solution in the felling of a problem tree.

1994 *Farm Labourer,* MR. JAMES BARBER – FARMER, JOHNSON'S FIREWOOD
- Effectively performed daily farm chores.
- Assisted in repairs to heavy equipment.
- Performed a variety of repairs to smaller farm equipment.
- Operated all types of farm-related equipment.
- Operated wood chipper and chain saw.

EDUCATION

1994–present, *Heavy Equipment Technician,* SIR SANFORD FLEMING COLLEGE
- Obtained diploma as Heavy Equipment Technician:
  - Core coursework included hydraulics, power trains, engines, fuels and lubricants, welding, and mobile electrical systems;
  - Additional areas of study included human relations, environmental issues, preventive maintenance, and correct safety techniques.

Member of the School of Natural Resources Heavy Equipment Club.

Excellent references available on request.

Resume written by Bill Lozza

ROGER C. PRITCHARD

900 - 17th Street • Imperial Beach, CA 91932 • (619) 987-6543

OBJECTIVE: A position in Technical Sales.

> Roger shows how his Navy recruiting talents are transferable to civilian sales.

SUMMARY

Award-winning Navy Recruiter with in-depth experience in sales, marketing, prospecting and network development. Highly successful communicator and closer. Consistently exceeded monthly and annual quotas by up to 240%. Solid technical and supervisory background. Dedicated to top quality customer service.

PROFESSIONAL EXPERIENCE, U.S. Navy, 1976–Present

Recruiting Sales

Successfully completed a 180-hour course covering sales and marketing techniques (Naval Recruiting School), including prospecting; marketing; product/service information; and closing. As a Recruiter/Canvasser, built prospect list through community research; cold calling; public contact; and canvassing of likely sources, including schools, local businesses, and career counselors. Effectively communicated Navy features and benefits to prospects. Painted verbal pictures to contrast the advantages of buying the product (the Navy) versus the disadvantages of not buying.

- Led district recruiting force in sales, consistently exceeding monthly quota by 25–40%.
- Over a one-year period, exceeded district monthly contract average by over 240%.
- Ranked number one of 69 production recruiters.
- Named Recruiter of the Year in 1990.
- Awarded the Navy Achievement Medal as approved by the Secretary of the Navy for excellence in recruiting.

Communication/Marketing

Generated leads by presenting public service talks at schools and civic organizations. Distributed marketing materials. Contacted students nearing high school graduation, as well as recent graduates, via direct mail. Developed a network of referral sources, including school counselors, current recruits awaiting departure and business owners.

- Proved extremely effective in direct public interaction, consistently setting appointments with 25% of all contacts.
- Through on-going positive client relations, maintained zero percent monthly loss rate (cancellations) versus the district average of 13%. This is especially significant because the time from closing until recruits report to boot camp can span up to one year.

Management/Technical

As a Navy Construction Mechanic, managed, motivated and trained teams of up to 50 employees. Responsibilities included: performance counseling and evaluation, shift scheduling, and workload distribution. Developed professional training materials and delivered lectures. Provided career development information based on extensive knowledge of Navy career programs. Assisted in managing a $600,000 budget.

Maintained, diagnosed and repaired a wide range of construction and material handling equipment, as well as truck/automotive systems. In-depth expertise in the following: gas/diesel engines; power trains; chassis and component assemblies; hydraulic valves and cylinders; fuel injection systems; general/special purpose test equipment; electrical systems; ignition systems; hydraulic/air vacuum braking systems.

EDUCATION

- Naval Recruiting School, U.S. Navy, 1995, (180 hours).
- Construction Mechanic School (Basic & Advanced), U.S. Navy, 1993, (960 hours).
- Leadership and Management Training, U.S. Navy, 1990, (80 hours).

Resume written by Lynn Vincent

Gregory I. Kessler

Box 105,
Wurtsmith AFB, MI 48753
(517) 987-6543

Gregory aims for a civilian job similar to his Air Force position, and eliminates any military jargon.

OBJECTIVE

A position as Emergency Generator Installation and Field Maintenance Technician with a government contractor.

SUMMARY OF QUALIFICATIONS

- Significant experience in prime power plant operations and electrical power plant equipment.
- Skill in interpreting technical publications, blueprints, and schematic wiring and connections diagrams.
- Expertise in electrical and electronic installation, maintenance, and troubleshooting.
- Experience in repairing gasoline and diesel engines, generator alternators and exciters, centrifuges, starter motors, and other associated generating and distributing equipment.

RELEVANT EXPERIENCE

United States Air Force 1981–present
POWER PLANT OPERATOR

- Operated, maintained, inspected and repaired prime and emergency generator sets rated at 3KW to 3000KW.
- Operated electrical switch gear components such as switches, power transfer controls, circuit breakers and rheostats.
- Controlled the distribution of electrical power to buses and feeder circuits.
- Monitored and analyzed readings from instruments such as ammeters, voltmeters, frequency meters, temperature and pressure-indicating devices.
- Inspected and operated auxiliary equipment such as air compressors, cooling water pumps and heat exchangers.
- Prevented a complete power outage at Shemya AFB, AK: discovered an extremely hot on-line compressor producing low operating pressure; immediately started the standby air compressor to replenish the air system, prior to shutting down the failed compressor.

POWER EQUIPMENT MAINTENANCE MECHANIC

- Operated, maintained, and repaired diesel- and gasoline-engine driven generator sets and other associated equipment, the size of which ranged from 1.5 to 100 kilowatts.
- Increased resistance against the acid spray from batteries by coating the generator battery containers with a fiberglass adhesive. This resulted in a reduction of hours spent sanding, scraping, and repainting the containers, and enabled them to last up to six months longer.

– Continued –

RELEVANT EXPERIENCE, Continued	**POWER EQUIPMENT MAINTENANCE MECHANIC**, continued

- Assisted and instructed the Brevard County Sheriff's Department in the installation of two MB-19 generators for use at their transmitter sites and SWAT team training areas.
- Diagnosed the problem of a MEP-003 generator set that failed to supply output voltage. Ordered and replaced the part and restored the unit to full operation in record time.
- Ensured the safety of personnel and prevented a fire in their living quarters by immediately responding to an electrical short and successfully rewiring the system.

SPECIFIC EQUIPMENT EXPERIENCE

EMERGENCY GENERATION SETS: Onan, DMT Corp., Marathon Electric, KATO Engineering, GENERAC, and KOHLER (Military Models: USAF FERMONT MB-TEEN and MEP Series).

ENGINES: Cummins, Caterpillar, Detroit Diesel, and Waukesha.

AUTOMATIC TRANSFER PANELS: Onan, Russelectric, KOHLER, and GENERAC.

EDUCATION

A.A. degree in Electrical and Mechanical Technology, currently pursuing through CCAF. Expected graduation February 1996. (Current overall GPA: 3.2))

Diesel Engine Overhaul School, Sheppard AFB, Texas.

Technical Training with Onan and Cooper Industries.

HONORS & AWARDS

Air Force Achievement Medal for meritorious service.

3 Good Conduct Medals.

Letters of Appreciation.

ADDITIONAL INFORMATION

Calm and levelheaded under extremely adverse conditions. Self-motivated and dependable under any and all conditions. Willing to relocate.

REFERENCES

Available on request.

Resume written by Therrall Haygood

JOSEPH NAVARONE

1000 Fifth Street • Smithtown, MA 02566 • (222) 453-7005

OBJECTIVE

A position as an electronics technician, with a career goal of advancement to an electrical engineer.

PERSONAL PROFILE

- Highly skilled electronic technician with exceptional trouble-shooting and repair capabilities.
- Quick learner; honor student recognized for achieving superior scholastic achievement (98%) in completing an accelerated course of instruction.
- Demonstrated ability to supervise personnel; noted as an "exceptional leader and resourceful manager."
- Knowledgeable regarding IBM-PC compatible hardware and WordPerfect, Word Star, Form Tool, Windows, Windows Works, and Networking software.

PROFESSIONAL EXPERIENCE

Electronics Technician, U.S. NAVY, 1990–present

- Performed highly technical trouble-shooting for scheduled and unscheduled maintenance and repair, of electronic communication and aviation in-flight navigation and detection systems, including:
  - Radar Systems
  - Radar Altimeters
  - Infrared Devices
  - Recorder Systems
  - Radar and Tactical Displays
  - Doppler Navigation Equipment
  - Communication Systems
  - Electronic Countermeasures Equipment
  - IFF/SIF Equipment
  - Analog Computing Devices
  - Radio Navigation Equipment
  - Digital Data Systems.
- Competently operated the following equipment for maintenance and repair tasks:
  - Volt Ohm-Milliammeter
  - Signal Generator
  - Frequency Counter
  - Specialized System Test Equipment
  - Oscilloscope
  - Megger
- Interpreted schematics, block diagrams, and technical documents in performing maintenance and repair tasks.

Management and Training, U.S. NAVY, 1981–1989

- Supervised up to 16 technicians, directing production, safety, and efficient performance.
- Selected as Division Training Officer, a duty normally assigned to a senior level petty officer.
- Promoted subordinate development to enhance personnel and division productivity.
- Effectively counseled personnel in preparation for promotion exams, resulting in a 35% advancement rate.

HIGHLIGHTS OF ACCOMPLISHMENTS *As noted from performance evaluations*

- Directly contributed to the return of 3,500 items to the supply systems, resulting in $3.5 million worth of sorely needed materials available to the unit.
- Restructured the division training format, achieving a 45% increase in personnel qualifications/licensing.
- Initiated new procedures to improve the tracking of personnel qualifications and licensing.
- Instituted a training information database to simplify tracking of training efforts.
- Skillfully managed a $7.5K training budget while ensuring a cost-effective means of attaining and enhancing required skill levels.
- Successfully modified 3 fleet aircraft in support of Operation Desert Storm.

EDUCATION/TRAINING

- Completed over 1700 hours of military technical training in electronics; avionics technician.
- Enrolled at Smithtown Community College with plans to transfer to an electronic engineering program at a four-year university.

Resume written by Gilda Weisskopf

Luke Worcester

987 West Avenue
Langley AFB, WV 80023
(708) 987-6543

OBJECTIVE	A Management position in a Human Resources or an Administrative department.

SUMMARY

- Over 15 years' experience planning, initiating, organizing and managing programs.
- Effectively motivate individuals to accomplish a common goal.
- Proven ability to transform unfavorable programs and procedures.
- Get results that last.
- Able to make the unpopular but essential decisions.

EXPERIENCE

Management/Problem Solving

- Achieved 150% contribution on fund-raising event (Combined Federal Campaign).
- Increased dormitory facilities rating from unsatisfactory to excellent.
- Initiated Quality Control Program to review correspondence.
- Received several awards for meritorious service.
- Managed unit recognition and promotion programs.

Supervision

- Coordinated morale, welfare, and career progression of 300 personnel; over 75% have been promoted.
- Founded "Top Three" Council program which identifies top-notch officers in unit.

Administration/Communication

- Initiated Unit Advisory Council, which bridges communication gap between enlisted and non-enlisted personnel.
- Wrote quality control performance reports.
- Outlined operating instructions for proper administrative procedures for entire complex.
- Authored commendation letters to personnel.

Community/Public Relations

- Active in sports programs.
- Spearheaded increased canned food donations for needy families during Christmas program.
- Coordinated staff picnic program.

WORK HISTORY

1986–present	**Chief Master Sergeant,** E9
	United States Air Force – Langley AFB, WV
1977–1986	**Technical Sergeant,** E6, USAF – George AFB, CA
1971–1977	**Senior Airman,** E3, USAF – Travis AFB, CA

EDUCATION

A.A., Electronics Technology; El Camino College, Carson, CA
Management Training at Senior NCO Academy

Resume written by Cynthia Mackey

Action Verbs

The **<u>underlined</u>** words are especially good for pointing out **accomplishments**.

Management Skills
administered
analyzed
assigned
<u>attained</u>
chaired
consolidated
contracted
coordinated
delegated
developed
directed
evaluated
executed
<u>improved</u>
<u>increased</u>
organized
oversaw
planned
prioritized
produced
recommended
reviewed
scheduled
<u>strengthened</u>
supervised

Communication Skills
addressed
arbitrated
arranged
authored
collaborated
<u>convinced</u>
corresponded
developed
directed
drafted
edited
enlisted
formulated
influenced
interpreted
lectured
mediated

Communication *(continued)*
moderated
negotiated
persuaded
promoted
publicized
reconciled
recruited
spoke
translated
wrote

Research Skills
clarified
collected
critiqued
diagnosed
evaluated
examined
extracted
identified
inspected
interpreted
interviewed
investigated
organized
reviewed
summarized
surveyed
systematized

Technical Skills
assembled
built
calculated
computed
configured
designed
devised
engineered
fabricated
installed
maintained
operated
<u>overhauled</u>

Technical *(continued)*
performed trouble-
    shooting
programmed
remodeled
repaired
retrieved
solved
<u>upgraded</u>

Teaching Skills
adapted
advised
clarified
coached
communicated
coordinated
demystified
developed
enabled
encouraged
evaluated
explained
facilitated
guided
informed
instructed
persuaded
set goals
stimulated
trained

Clerical or Detail Skills
approved
arranged
catalogued
classified
collected
compiled
executed
generated
implemented
inspected
monitored
operated

Clerical *(continued)*
organized
prepared
processed
purchased
recorded
retrieved
screened
specified
systematized
tabulated
validated

Helping Skills
assessed
assisted
clarified
coached
counseled
demonstrated
diagnosed
educated
<u>expedited</u>
facilitated
guided
motivated
referred
rehabilitated
represented

Financial Skills
administered
allocated
analyzed
appraised
audited
balanced
budgeted
calculated
computed
developed
forecast
managed
marketed
planned
projected
researched

Creative Skills
acted
conceptualized
created
customized
designed
developed
directed
established
fashioned
<u>founded</u>
illustrated
<u>initiated</u>
instituted
integrated
<u>introduced</u>
<u>invented</u>
<u>originated</u>
performed
planned
<u>revitalized</u>
shaped

More Verbs for Accomplishments
<u>achieved</u>
<u>expanded</u>
<u>improved</u>
<u>pioneered</u>
<u>reduced</u> (losses)
<u>resolved</u> (problems)
<u>restored</u>
<u>spearheaded</u>
<u>transformed</u>

Examples of some

Skill Areas

TRANSFERABLE SKILLS and SPECIAL KNOWLEDGE

The areas of Skill and Knowledge you choose to present on your resume are determined by what you think will be required of you in your new line of work. Here are some examples of Skill Areas presented by job hunters, for the jobs they were seeking. (Remember, these are some POSSIBLE skill areas for those jobs—not necessarily the RIGHT ones for anybody else!)

The job: **School Counselor**
The skill areas presented:
—Individual Counseling
—Testing and Evaluation
—Group Counseling
—Resource Development
—Career Development

The job: **Research Chemist**
The skill areas presented:
—Quality Control
—Project Management
—Analysis/R&D
—Instrument Knowledge

The job: **Substitute Teacher**
(in an inner city school district)
The skill areas presented:
—Teaching
—Planning and Organizing
—Cultural/Racial Exposure
—Expertise in Math, Science, Health

The job: **Program Development**
(with an elderly population)
The skill areas presented:
—Administration and Planning
—Elderly Services
—Community Services

The job: **Family Mediator**
The skill areas presented:
—Conflict Resolution
—Counseling and Interviewing
—Teaching and Educating

The job: **Fitness Consultant**
The skill areas presented:
—Athletic Training
—Individual Consultations
—Fitness Program Design and
    Implementation
—Personal Accomplishments
    (relevant awards won)

The job: **Marketing and Public Relations**
The skill areas presented:
—Promotion
—Marketing
—Public Relations
—Customer Service/Needs Assessment

The job: **Sales Representative or Manufacturer's Rep**
The skill areas presented:
—Effective Sales Techniques
—Market Development
—Presentation/Communication

The job: **Commercial Leasing Agent**
The skill areas presented:
—Sales and Marketing
—Business Contacts
—Contract Negotiation
—Facilities Management

The job: **Receptionist**
The skill areas presented:
—Office Experience
—Telephone and Communication Skills
—Computer Knowledge

The job: **Private Investigator**
The skill areas presented:
—Investigation
—Case Management
—Security Consultation

The job: **Union Business Agent**
The skill areas presented:
—Contract Negotiations
—Grievance Handling and Contract
    Enforcement
—Organizing Workers
—Administration/Management

The job: **Information Specialist**
The skill areas presented:
—Information Needs Analysis
—Advising
—Research and Writing
—Data Management

The job: **Firefighter**
(in a city fire department)
The skill areas presented:
—Crisis Evaluation and Response
—PR, Community Relations
—Medical Teamwork
—Training and Quality Assurance

The job: **Service Writer**
(for an auto manufacturer)
The skill areas presented:
—Needs Assessment/Public Relations
—Technical Knowledge
—Business Management

The job: **Parish Minister**
The skill areas presented:
—Counseling and Pastoral Service
—Religious Education
—Worship
—Administration

The job: **Wardrobe Assistant**
(with a movie company)
The skill areas presented:
—Managing Dressing Room
—Appointments/Logistics
—Costume Maintenance
—Bookkeeping, Shopping, Errands

The job: **Accountant**
(with a computer firm)
The skill areas presented:
—Bookkeeping
—Computerized Accounting
—Computer Systems and Applications

The job: **Regional Planner**
The knowledge areas presented:
—Land Use
—Transportation
—Planning
—Economic Development

The job: **Massage Therapist**
(freelancing with a fitness center)
The skill areas presented:
—Non-Invasive Pain Control
—Sports Massage/Sports Therapy
—Assessment and Client Reeducation
—Professional Affiliations and Referrals

The job: **Program Administrator**
The skill areas presented:
—Administration/Management
—Program Development
—Special Projects
—Community Relations

The job: **Investigative Assistant**
The skill areas presented:
—Research
—Report Writing and Documentation
—Interviewing
—Data Entry

The job: **Staff Accountant**
The skill areas presented:
—Tax Planning
—Advising Management
—Trouble-Shooting
—Computer Conversion

The job: **Social Worker**
The skill areas presented:
—Clinical Counseling
—Assessment and Diagnosis
—Supervision/Administration
—Group Counseling
—Program Development

The job: **Doctor's Receptionist**
The skill areas presented:
—Office Skills
—Client Screening
—Client Relations

The job: **Assistant Manager Trainee**
(in a restaurant)
The skill areas presented:
—Business Management
—Personnel, Supervision, Training
—Food Handling, Preparation, and
    Presentation

Worksheet/Guide for a Recommendation Letter

■ **Instructions to the job hunter:** Make some photocopies of this blank form so you'll have one for each person you ask to write a recommendation letter. **Then carefully fill in the blanks below, attach a copy of your resume, and give the worksheet and resume to the person you asked to write a recommendation letter** (same as a "reference letter"). Once **YOU fill in the blanks**, this form will become a helpful GUIDE for your reference person for writing an effective recommendation letter for you.

Remember: if you request recommendation letters from several people, *each form you fill in will be a little different* because the information you write down depends on your relationship with *that* person.

■ **Instructions FROM the job-hunter TO the person writing the recommendation letter:**

The information below is provided to make it easier to write a recommendation letter for me.

My name _____ Date the letter is needed _____

Name, title and company of the potential employer who will get the recommendation letter:

_____

1. In the first paragraph, **state that this is a letter of recommendation for:**

   _____ (my name), who is seeking a position as:

   _____

   (job title, or kind of work sought)

2. In the second paragraph, **state the nature of our relationship** (supervisor, colleague, long-time personal friend, teacher, etc.), **how LONG you've known me, and the nature of the work, projects or other experience that we shared**—for example:

   Relationship: _____ Length of time known: _____

   Nature of the work or project: _____

   _____

3. In the third paragraph, **mention some of my skills, talents, abilities, or personal qualities, and describe one or two primary accomplishments** that you think would be interesting to the new employer because they demonstrate the skills needed for the work I'm now seeking—for example:

   A skill or ability important to the new job: _____

   A skill or ability important to the new job: _____

   A skill or ability important to the new job: _____

   An accomplishment that illustrates those skills: _____

   An accomplishment that illustrates those skills: _____

   (More on back of page if necessary) **(Note:** *The job hunter should point out the relevant skills and some accomplishments they'd like mentioned, but the reference person is the one who actually writes the letter.)*

4. In the last paragraph, if you are willing to be called by the potential employer, **state how you can be reached for more information.**

Finally, please give me a call at _____ and I'll pick up the completed letter and deliver it to the employer. THANK YOU.

© Damn Good Resume Service

Cover Letters

Your resume should always have a good COVER LETTER attached, as a personal communication between you and the individual who receives the resume.

Most people are intimidated by this task, but it's not that hard if you think of it as just a **friendly, simple communication from one person** (who's looking for a good job) **to another** (who's looking for a good employee). It is in the interests of both parties to make a good connection!

How To Write a Good Cover Letter

1. **Be sure to address it**—by name and title—**to the person who could hire you**. When it's *impossible* to learn their name, use their functional title, such as "Dear Manager." You may have to guess ("Dear Selection Committee") but *never* say "To whom it may concern" or "Dear Sir or Madam"!

2. **Show that you know a little about the company**, that you are aware of their current problems, interests, or priorities.

3. **Express your enthusiasm and interest** in this line of work and this company. If you have a good idea that might help the employer resolve a problem currently facing their industry, offer to come in and discuss it.

4. **Project warmth and friendliness,** while still being professional. Avoid any generic phrases such as "Enclosed please find..." *This is a letter to a real live person!*

5. **Set yourself apart from the crowd.** Identify at least one thing about you that's unique—say a special talent for getting along with everybody at work, or some unusual skill that goes beyond the essential requirements of the position—something that distinguishes you AND is relevant to the job. (Then, if several others are equally qualified for the job, your uniqueness may be the reason to choose YOU.)

6. **Be specific** about what you are asking for and what you are offering. Make it clear which position you're applying for and just what experience or skill you have that relates to that position.

7. **Take the initiative** about the next step whenever possible, and be specific. "I'll call your office early next week to see if we could meet soon and discuss this job opening," for example. OR—if you're exploring for UN-announced jobs that my come up—"I'll call your office next week to see if we could meet soon, to discuss your company's needs for help in the near future."

8. **Keep it brief**—a few short paragraphs, all on one page.

Sample Cover Letters

NOTE: The DATE and the job hunter's RETURN ADDRESS AND PHONE NUMBER have been removed from the sample letters that follow in order to save space. *Thanks to JENNY MISH, who wrote the last three of these cover letters.*

Marjorie Lawrence, Director
Professional Training Institute
3056 Hildegard Ave.
Richmond, CA 94806

SEE RESUME ON PAGE 34

Dear Ms. Lawrence,
The position of Marketing Trainer that you described in our meeting is an opportunity of great motivational and professional dimensions. I can envision a strong team atmosphere, working to achieve the Institute's goals, with an emphasis on commitment to the representatives' growth potential.

My attached resume will show that I have a strong training background. I believe I have a great deal to contribute to the department, given my experience and interest, as well as my sense of humor and creative energy.

I am very excited about the position. The people, functions, and environment all add up to a very appealing challenge. I look forward to talking with you in person.

Sincerely,
Maria Doshan

STGC
Box 1282
41 Sutter St.
San Francisco, CA 94104

SEE RESUME ON PAGE 42

Dear Selection Committee:
Because of my combined interest in accounting and computers, I am applying for the bookkeeper position which you recently advertised.

I am enclosing a copy of my resume for your consideration, and would like to call your attention to the areas of skill and achievement in my background that are most relevant.

• Over 12 years bookkeeping experience for various businesses.
• Four years experience with computerized accounting systems.
• Thoroughly familiar with PC-DOS operating system.
• Exceptionally organized and resourceful; wide range of skills.

My present employer is gradually retiring from active law practice, and therefore I am looking for a new position. My current salary is $40,000 and I look to upgrade in my next job.

I would appreciate a personal interview with you to discuss my application further.

Sincerely,
Kate Dietrich

Coordinator of Personnel
938 Missouri Blvd.
Oakland, CA 94606

SEE RESUME ON PAGE 40

Dear Coordinator,
I was very pleased to learn of the opening for the position of Principal at your high school.

On my enclosed resume I have outlined my professional and educational background, and given special attention to those experiences and accomplishments that address your school's stated needs and requirements.

I am a "take charge" type of administrator, and have demonstrated strong leadership and initiative in addressing the schools' most difficult problems. I have a particularly strong record of success in developing curricula that meet the needs of all students.

It is my nature and philosophy to look for the best in students, and to do whatever is necessary to help them perform to their fullest potential. With this in mind, I recently attended a workshop at Harvard University (and plan to return this summer), where materials have been developed to effectively teach study skills to high school students. This workshop prepared me to introduce these critically important materials to teachers for use in their classrooms.

I would welcome the opportunity to share with you additional examples of contributions I might make to the program at your school, and I will call later this week to see if we can arrange an appointment.

Sincerely,
Ruben Perez

Sharon Reeves, Recycling Program Manager
San Francisco Recycling Program
90005 Market Street, Suite 501
San Francisco, CA 94103

Dear Ms. Reeves,
I am interested in applying for the Commercial Recycling Coordinator position currently open in your department.

As one of the Bay Area's most experienced recycling managers, I believe I have a lot to offer. I have worked extensively with commercial and institutional organizations to audit and reduce waste, and I have been instrumental in the design and implementation of numerous recycling programs. I would be pleased to work with you to continue San Francisco's reputation for national leadership in recycling and waste management.

I hope you agree that I would be an asset to your staff, and I would like the opportunity to interview with you for the position. I plan to call your office early next week to explore this possibility with you.

Sincerely,
Tania Hillegass

Cathy Columbo
Director of Operations, U.S.
Giorgio Asante
988 Fifth Avenue
New York, NY 10011

Dear Ms. Asante,
I am eager to introduce myself as a potential employee of Giorgio Asante.

I have been an enthusiastic and loyal follower of Giorgio Asante designs for over ten years, and I would love to work at the new store in San Francisco when it opens next fall.

My ten years of experience as a wholesale apparel marketing and production assistant has exposed me to many facets of the clothing industry, and has heightened my appreciation for the aesthetics and standards of Giorgio Asante. I am pleased to present myself as a very effective salesperson who is committed to total customer satisfaction.

I believe that my fierce loyalty, broad experience, and strong desire to learn would make me a valuable asset to your staff. I will call you next week to answer any questions you may have, and to learn about Giorgio Asante's staffing needs for the new San Francisco store.

Sincerely,
Beverly Proctor

Jane Alexander
Career Planning and Placement Center
U.C. Berkeley
2200 Bancroft Way
Berkeley, CA 94720

Dear Ms. Alexander,
I am a re-entry student, interested in career development and marketing. I am excited about the possibility of working at the Career Planning and Placement Center as Student Affairs Officer. I know that I would be very good at promoting the Center and U.C. Berkeley students for purposes of job development with potential employers.

An extremely creative and dynamic person, I have twelve years of experience promoting ideas and services by initiating contact and working effectively with professionals from varying backgrounds. I am extremely resourceful and I have very strong verbal and written communication skills. I am comfortable making public presentations for persuasive or informative purposes. In addition, I have worked with young adults for several years and am well aware of their special strengths and needs.

My resume is enclosed, and I will follow up with a call to your office within a week. In the meantime, if you wish to call me I can be reached any evening at 510-220-9998,

Sincerely,
Anita Corrigan

THE ACID TEST

What Do Employers Think About Resumes?

To test the effectiveness of our resumes, we asked a panel of San Francisco Bay Area employers to give us some feedback.

These are the seven resumes reviewed by the employers:

Kate (bookkeeper), page 42
Maria (health plan rep/trainer), pages 34-35
John (waiter/electronics tech), page 36
Josephine (supermarket checker), page 37
Robert (gardener/park supervisor), pages 38-39
Ruben (high school principal), pages 40-41
Lorraine (college grad/researcher), page 45

The employers on our panel were:

"DC" is an employment recruiter for a bank with thousands of employees.

"JD" is director of training programs at a community career center employing five people.

"KJ" is a recruiter for county civil service jobs in hospitals, clinics, and health agencies.

"MM" recruits professionals for an engineering-related company with 11,000 employees.

"RS" is a personnel and training director for a software company with 200 employees.

"RV" is executive director of a small nonprofit agency.

"SP" recruits for a construction company with 50,000 employees worldwide.

"AA" hires local staff for a large toy manufacturer and distributor.

"SB" hires secretaries, janitors, and maintenance staff for a large pharmaceutical firm with 10,000 employees.

As you read, you may want to refer back to the employer profiles above for perspective on their views.

You'll notice how differently employers approach resumes! Some look at them conservatively, others with a "guerrilla tactics" approach. Some like specific objectives, others prefer general. Perhaps the most controversial area is the subjective, self-marketing statements—employers either love 'em or they hate 'em.

And notice that EMPLOYERS DON'T ALWAYS AGREE. So you obviously can't please everybody all the time! On the other hand, THIS panel is virtually unanimous on some points—for example, they're all turned off by pretentious, commercially prepared resumes.

Notice, too, that although each of these seven sample resumes WORKED to get an interview for the job hunter, employers still found some areas that could be improved, in addition to the things they liked.

1. HOW DO YOU DECIDE WHETHER IT'S A GOOD RESUME?

DC: The objective is the key; that gets it to the right person, the appropriate hiring manager. It also needs to look nice, as though you've taken some time with it. And keep it to one or two pages.

JD: The most important thing is to focus on what you're seeking. And show that you understand the main qualifications of the job, rather than just showing your past job experience. Make it easy for the recruiter—don't use jargon that the average lay person can't understand.

KJ: The format and presentation are important; and show what functions you have performed, along with your job history.

MM: Conciseness—a resume that makes for quick reading and that supports your interest areas; also that shows you take pride in your work.

RS: I look for how easy it is to read, how apparent the qualifications are in a quick scan. The objective needs to stand out.

RV: Is it targeted to the job and to the most critical skill area of the job? It should take the reader by the hand: "This is what I've done and where I've done it, and these are the achievements to back up what I'm applying for."

SB: It needs to look good on the page, and have a pretty specific objective, otherwise, I won't read it. I also don't read it if it says, "Looking for a position with a company that will allow me to use wonderful, fabulous skills." Instead, I want to see "Looking for a middle management position in finance," etc.

SP: I look for experience (particularly experience with the competition) and a good education.

AA: I go by its general appearance—also the specific qualifications for the position being recruited.

2. WHAT MAKES YOU DECIDE THAT THIS LOOKS LIKE SOMEBODY YOU WOULD LIKE TO INTERVIEW?

DC: If I see action words and accomplishments rather than just job descriptions, that's when I get excited about interviewing. Also if there's something in the cover letter that attracts my attention, that shows time and thought and effort, and some real interest in our organization.

JD: If the person is very sure of what they want to do and what contribution they can make. Our bank needs self-starters, so we're looking for demonstrated initiative.

KJ: If the skills and functions on the resume are appropriate and well presented.

MM: If the education and experience are a good match for the position we have open. [AA agrees.]

RS: The person's background looks good and there are no big gaps in their history. I like to see clear objectives, qualifications, and continuity in the job history. (If you took time off, then clearly state the reason.)

RV: Show that you know the lingo of the environment; for example, in sales, show that you know how to close.

SB: The resume writer has no control over this because our candidates have to meet a manager's particular requirements—for example, having worked with the "Big Eight" or having an MBA.

With secretaries it's not so cut-and-dried; then I'll look for skills listed at the top of the resume: typing, shorthand, software packages, etc., and then look at the job history to see if she's a job hopper. (Of course things are changing—because people get laid off.)

SP: I pay the most attention when the objective is for a specific position that relates to the job hunter's skills.

3. WHAT DO YOU CONSIDER MOST IMPORTANT ON A RESUME?

DC: The objective. Plus dates when things happened, and accomplishments.

JD: Knowing what you want to do and what contribution you could make.

KJ: Valid information in an easy-to-read, attractive style.

RS: A clear objective, backed up with qualifying experience and continuity in the work history.

RV: Realizing that the employer is looking for "red flags" and making sure there aren't any; cover gaps in dates, cover duties, eliminate suspicions and questions.

SB: The presentation and the objective.

SP: The address and phone number! Lots of people only put them in the cover letter!

AA: Meeting the qualifications for the job.

4. WHAT TURNS YOU OFF ON A RESUME?

DC: Personal data—that's a major "red flag." Typos, inconsistent punctuation, lack of address and phone number. And huge paragraphs that look like job descriptions, without any skills and accomplishments pulled out.

JD: Those odd-size resumes from resume services, saying "Presenting the candidacy of . . ." Also personal information, and resumes that sound like job descriptions. Also, not looking at the employer's needs, not doing any research.

KJ: Those portfolio things on parchment paper, from a resume service. They look so fake and phony, an instant turnoff.

MM: Omissions in terms of dates, and misspellings.

RS: Long cover letters and resumes more than two pages long.

RV: Excess cosmetics, substituting form for content. It should look nice, but don't go overboard; it's a traditional tool and it should look traditional.

SB: Resumes that open like a book, saying "Presenting so-and-so," done by a commercial resume service. They're just a rip-off and I don't even read them anymore.

SP: A photo; I have to remove them because a manager should be color blind and gender blind. Also not sending the resume to the right place.

AA: Misspelled words, poor grammar, a messy look.

5. WHAT WOULD YOU LIKE TO SEE DIFFERENT ON RESUMES THAT WOULD HELP EMPLOYERS IDENTIFY A GOOD CANDIDATE?

DC: I want to see people doing a good selling job talking about what they've done and accomplished. And I want to get the essence of the person, a feeling for their personality. (Sometimes people are too regimented as to what they think they "should" be saying about themselves.)

JD: Fewer chronological resumes. Less about job history and more about skills that apply to the job.

KJ: Resumes that are easy to read and understand, and that validate your background.

MM: Being real candid about what responsibility you've held, and what you're proud of accomplishing in that position. That lets me see where your values are. Also conciseness. (People have a misconception about resumes; they're really just a tickler, not the place to give the whole story away.)

RS: Resumes on one page, or 1½ at most—brief and concise.

RV: I'd like to see job hunters incorporate their problem-solving skills right into the resume. For example, "We had a problem with attendance and this is what we did to resolve it." That's probably a little visionary, but it would give me an idea of how they think and what their management style is.

SB: Don't be too splashy. There's nothing wrong with good white paper; in fact it's better because it makes better copies. Be honest and clear, and be grammatically correct and consistent.

AA: In the employment history I'd like to see the months included along with the years. And no highlights section—just the objective, education, and experience.

SP: Be honest and give some objective information rather than subjective self-evaluation.

6. HOW WOULD YOU REACT TO ANY OF THESE SEVEN JOB HUNTERS' RESUMES IF YOU WERE HIRING FOR THAT KIND OF WORK? DO YOU HAVE ANY COMMENTS, PRO OR CON?

JOHN's resume, page 36

DC: I like the highlights; they mention his professional manner with customers and then the skill section goes on to show how he has done this. This approach highlights a person's strengths and style and can work for almost everybody.

JD: It's easy to read and very clear.

KJ: I'd rather see his highlights in a cover letter when they include subjective things such as interpersonal skills, because the cover letter is the appropriate place for a sales pitch. I like that it's one page and gives me functions and skills.

MM: I like the objective. I'd suggest pushing the education up to the top. (I'd probably call him first to see why, all of a sudden, he wants to make this move; then if that made sense, I'd schedule him for a test.)

RS: I like it on one page. He should move the education and training to the top because most of his work was in restaurant management. In the job history, I'd change it to "1976–present: Consultant" or "1976–91: Waiter," and "1991–95: Consultant to Restaurant Management." These are guerrilla or street-fight tactics.

SB: I'd recommend putting the education up nearer to the objective; and of course including a good cover letter.

JOSEPHINE's resume, page 37

JD: This resume is right on target because it answers my questions with relevant skill areas presented in a hierarchy—customer service, supervision, and then administration. The objective is short, concise, and specific. And the summary tells me the qualities that relate to the three areas listed below: it shows that she's honest and reliable and productive, and consistently pleasant to customers.

KJ: I like it. Very tight, attractive format, and the skills are clearly pulled out. I like the "summary of qualifications" better than "highlights of qualifications" elsewhere.

MM: If everybody could do a resume on one page it would be perfect.

RS: I don't think she needs a functional resume.

RV: I appreciate the amount of white space.

AA: Good appearance.

SP: Very good layout.

KATE's resume, page 42

DC: It's important to back up the objective, and Kate does that when she talks about her computer expertise. I also like to see it all on one page like that.

JD: I like this resume a lot. I especially like the reduced type here because you can see all the information without turning the page.

KJ: I like seeing the skills pulled out like this, rather than having to go through a work chronology and have to figure out what her skills are.

MM: It helps a lot, from the interviewer's perspective, that she goes into detail about what she knows and doesn't know. I like the layout and also the more specific objective. I'd have trouble with the number of positions she's listed and I'd want to cover that question with her right away.

SP: The overall layout leads you through it. I like seeing the computer experience that's appropriate to the job. And it's good to see the continuing education under her college degree.

   The work history is clear, though it's a bit scattered and I'd probably call her up to see if she's been laid off or was moving to improve her salary.

MARIA's resume, pages 34–35

JD: It's easy to read and very clear; she has kept her extensive background concise by using a functional resume.

KJ: She could use smaller type and get it all on one page so I could see everything at one time. The objective is too limited, and I'd rather see that in a cover letter.

MM: I like it, even though it's different from my style in that it's so specific to one company. I like the highlights and the one-liners—really concise. What she brings out on the first page is nailed down on the second page.

SB: I don't like the comment "Keen intuition; warm, sincere, down-to-earth teaching style." But I do like "Designed and presented seminars for hospital middle managers;" it's honest, it's something she actually DID, and it's objective information rather than subjective self-evaluation. I've never liked highlights. I like the old-fashioned kind of resume. I want to know where and when you did something.

   Don't put in irrelevant information—for example, Maria's dramatics teaching. In the corporate world I've learned there's no connection between training and teaching.

ROBERT's resume, pages 38–39

RS: I think this resume has too much information—it should be readable in 30 seconds.

MM: The directed objective looks solid. I would switch the "park technical experience" to the front, but find this resume very interesting. [Editor's note: We took MM's advice and moved "park technical experience" from page two to page one.]

RUBEN's resume, pages 40–41

RS: This is a good example in terms of quick readability. Ruben is using what I call "guerrilla tactics" in not emphasizing his latest jobs, but focusing on the three years at North High School. (You can also emphasize one part of your experience if you're going for a job change that requires that experience.) Ruben could make a brief comment to explain why he went into corporate management.

DC: It's good that he has stressed what's important to him. I'm not sure it makes sense for him to do his resume in a chronological style—it's not as smooth as the others. On the other hand it looks good and says what he wants to get across. It's maybe too slanted toward his assistant principal job.

MM: I like it a lot—this is more my style. I like the combination format; it's a nice way to present himself, with the positions highlighted and also the action words in terms of what he's done.

KJ: The one-liners seem to take up too much space. I don't want to go through a chronology and have to figure out what the skills are; I'd rather see the skills pulled out like they are on Kate's or Josephine's resumes.

SB: Putting the education first is a good idea.

AA: Looks good; the combination format answers questions.

LORRAINE's resume, page 45

AA: I like this because it is a combination of both chronological and functional, with the skills for the position described. And it looks good. I'd like to see the skills for her last position also, and know whether she's still there. [Editor's note: Lorraine was still employed there at the time this resume was written.]

RS: Ideal—you can go right to the job history.

MM: Nice layout. I like the education at the end and "cum laude." It's good to show things you're proud of; it shows you like yourself.

MORE EMPLOYER COMMENTS AND ADVICE FOR JOB HUNTERS

FORMATS: FUNCTIONAL vs. CHRONOLOGICAL

RS: I don't like functional resumes because I want to know where a person did what. But a functional format is good if you've had lots of jobs. In that case, my idea would be to use a "guerrilla approach," i.e., drop jobs and extend others "as long as your rear is covered." The most important thing is "getting on the beach," getting an interview. It's important to present a good image, but don't lie about your skills—don't say you can do something you can't do.

SB: An organization of recruiters I belong to, PYRA, believes that you do a functional resume when you have something to hide. However, sometimes a functional resume is good when you're doing a career change—or when you need to emphasize a part of your experience where you indeed don't HAVE that much experience but you still want to move into that area. (I did that kind of resume myself. Still, I like the old-fashioned resume.)

JOB OBJECTIVES

RS: I like more general objectives ("using my skills in finance...") just in case there's both an accountant opening and another financial position.

SP: Don't make a generalized comment such as "desire challenging position." I will skip right over it. I pay the most attention when the objective is for a specific position based on the job hunter's skills.

MM: The more specific you are, the more likely you are to get what you want. The recruiter can then head you in the right direction.

COVER LETTERS

MM: I have a tendency to take a quick look at a resume and then go to the cover letter to see why they came to us, what they're interested in, what they're doing, so I can look at the resume in a more focused way. I use the cover letter to start seeing what kind of attitude a person has toward work.

SB: If there's anything unusual about your resume, you need to explain it in a cover letter. (I always read the ones with cover letters first.) A good cover letter could say, for example, "I've been an office manager for several years at one company but I don't want to put in so much overtime and I'm looking for a stable job in a stable company where I can work 8 to 5." Ordinarily I wouldn't interview someone for a secretarial job after they've been an office manager, but now she's telling me WHY, so I'll bring her in.

DC: A cover letter should highlight something about you or do something else to attract my attention. It should show time and thought and effort—like you're really interested in our organization.

OVERALL IMPRESSION

DC: A resume is a marketing tool, like a beautiful brochure, creating an image of professionalism. Real gut level, these resumes look nice, like someone has taken some time. They use a lot of action words with short sentences that say something—the ideal type of resume, all in two pages.

INDEX

RESUMES